DISCOVERING ANTIQUES

THE STORY OF WORLD ANTIQUES

GREYSTONE PRESS/NEW YORK · TORONTO · LONDON

This superb full-color work is brought to you in its entirety
from the original publisher, The British Publishing Corpora-
tion. Only the arrangement has been slightly altered. In fact,
rather than disturb the text in any way, you will find the
English monetary system used throughout the set. Here is a
handy conversion table showing the value of a Pound (£)
in terms of U.S. dollars.

DATES	U.S. Dollars equal to one Pound (£)
1939	$3.92 to 4.68
1940 to Sept. 1949	4.03
Sept. 1949 to Nov. 1967	2.80
Nov. 1967 to Aug. 1971	2.40
Aug. 1971 to June 1972	2.60
June 1972 to present	2.45 (floating rate)

20 shillings = one Pound (£)
21 shillings = one guinea

In February, 1971, the guinea was taken out of circulation.

TITLE PAGE PHOTO CREDIT: *Sauce-boat* by Bernard Palissy (1510-90), or
follower, first half of sixteenth century. Height 3¼ inches. (Victoria and
Albert Museum. Salting Bequest.)

Published by the Greystone Press
225 Park Avenue South
New York, N.Y. 10003

Library of Congress Catalog Card Number: 72-90688

Cover Design: Harold Franklin

MANUFACTURED IN THE UNITED STATES OF AMERICA.

Contents

Neville Williams

QUEEN VICTORIA'S PALACES

Fig. 1 (Frontispiece) **Queen Victoria** (1819–1901) by Bertha Müller, 1900, after H. von Angeli's original of 1899. Oil on canvas.
(National Portrait Gallery, London.)

Fig. 2 **Princess Victoria's Bedroom** at Kensington Palace, London.
On her eightieth birthday, Queen Victoria decided to restore the apartments she had occupied as a child to their original state. Of this Palace, she said: 'I have gone through painful and disagreeable scenes here, 'tis true, but I am still fond of the poor old palace'.
(By gracious permission of H.M. The Queen.)

As important to her for seclusion as for royal state occasions, Queen Victoria's palaces were as far apart as Scotland and the Isle of Wight

Queen Victoria was born in the Kensington Palace of Wren and Vanbrugh in 1819 in the suite of rooms assigned by George III to his fourth son Edward, Duke of Kent. He had come pounding across Europe with his duchess when her time drew nigh, so that their child might be born in England, even if theirs seemed a distant branch on the royal family tree.

It was at Kensington, amid the trees and grass, that the Princess spent her first eighteen years,

been in during her childhood and open them to the public; and so Kensington Palace has remained, for the royal suite, now forming part of the London Museum, displays many personal items and *objets d'art* of Victoria.

As Queen, she had inherited seven official residences. Besides Buckingham Palace, there were Windsor Castle, St. James's, Hampton Court, Kew, Holyrood House and Brighton Pavilion. The last, the Prince Regent's folly, Queen Victoria was to sell to the Brighton Town Commissioners in 1849.

Holyrood was in a dilapidated state and on her first visit to Edinburgh she ordered this 'princely and most beautiful place' to be renovated so that when she returned in 1852 she was able to sleep within the walls – the first monarch to do so since Charles I. The Dutch House at Kew, with much of

Fig. 3 *The 1855 Room* at *Buckingham Palace, London. This handsome room commemorates the visit of Napoleon III and the Empress Eugénie to England in 1855. They also went to Windsor, where the bed in which they slept, with its French eagle at the foot, may still be seen. (By gracious permission of H.M. The Queen.)*

Fig. 4 *The drawing-room, Balmoral Castle, near Aberdeen, drawing, late nineteenth century. In this view may be seen the extensive use that was made of tartan as a decorative motif.*

Radio Times Hulton Picture Library

sleeping every night in her mother's bedroom. Her father had died when she was five months old and her mother remained at daggers drawn with William IV, while the majordomo of the palace, Sir John Conroy, was always interfering and upsetting Fräulein Lehzen, the girl's governess. When King William paid a surprise visit to Kensington in 1836 he found that the Duchess of Kent had dared to take over the apartments on the floor above, always reserved for the sovereign and, worse, had partitioned the King's Gallery into separate rooms. No King has ever given the mother of the heir apparent a more severe reprimand than William IV gave to the Duchess.

In July 1837, a fortnight after her accession, Victoria left Kensington for good. 'Though I rejoice to go into Buckingham Palace', she wrote in her diary, 'it is not without feelings of regret that I shall bid adieu *for ever* to this my birthplace . . . I have gone through painful and disagreeable scenes here, 'tis true, but I still am fond of the poor old palace'. On her eighteenth birthday the Queen decided to restore the apartments there to the state they had

its gardens, she presented to the nation early in her reign, reserving for herself Queen's Cottage, where her parents' wedding-breakfast had been held. She subsequently made little use of it and in her Diamond Jubilee year gave this, also, to her people.

Cardinal Wolsey's Hampton Court had for fifty years been a 'grace and favour' residence instead of a sovereign's house, while St. James's was to remain a setting for court functions, such as *levées*. Effectively, then, Victoria had only two habitable houses – Windsor Castle and Buckingham Palace; once she became a mother she desperately needed holiday homes away from London and so she built Osborne, in the Isle of Wight, and Balmoral, in the Scottish Highlands.

Buckingham House had been bought by George III on his marriage, but it was his son who commissioned John Nash to transform it into a palace by virtual reconstruction. It was on so lavish a scale that the architect was dismissed by the Treasury on George IV's death, when his grandiose scheme was far from completion. Edward Blore took another seven years finishing the task so that the Palace was

5

Radio Times Hulton Picture Library

6

Mansell Collection

7

Crown copyright

Fig. 5 **Balmoral Castle,** *Aberdeen. Engraving by W. Banks & Son, Edinburgh.*
Acquired in 1848, Balmoral was one of Victoria's favourite retreats.

Fig. 6 **Buckingham Palace,** *Nash's reconstruction with the entrance through Marble Arch. Engraving, c.1840.*

Fig. 7 **Queen's Cottage,** *Kew. Victoria presented the Dutch House and gardens at Kew to the nation early in her reign, but retained this cottage until the year of her Diamond Jubilee.*

Fig. 8 **View of Sandringham House,** *Norfolk, by Albert Jenkins Humbert, c.1865. Water-colour. (Royal Institute of British Architects, London.)*

Fig. 9 **Queen Victoria's Bedroom** *in Osborne House, Isle of Wight. It was in this room that Victoria died, and it has been kept as she left it.*

ready for occupation just as William IV died.

Victoria's first impressions were favourable: 'I am much pleased with my rooms. They are high, pleasant and cheerful', she wrote, but soon she had compiled a list of defects. Eight years later, she wrote to the Prime Minister, Peel, pointing out the inconveniences of the Palace as a family home and her 'total want of accommodation'. If work was begun at once it could not be finished before early 1848, she said, when the Prince of Wales would be nearly seven and the Princess Royal nearly eight, 'and they cannot possibly be kept in the nursery any longer'. She also needed a room for entertaining far larger than anything available as well as adequate servants' quarters. At last, in 1847, Blore began the east front to complete the quadrangle, thus sealing off the open courtyard. The Queen waited until 1856 for her ballroom, designed by Sir James Pennethorne, which enabled the court 'drawing rooms' to be transferred from St. James's. There were no other structural changes during her reign, although the running of the Palace was completely reformed by the Prince Consort, following a detailed report by his old tutor, Baron Stockmar, who drew attention to the wasteful system and the lack of communication between the various departments – for instance, the Office of Woods and Forests cleaned the outsides of the windows, and the Lord Chamberlain's men cleaned the insides.

Bringing up children in London amid the glare of publicity became intolerable, and Victoria hankered after 'a place of one's own, quiet and retired', where long holidays could be enjoyed in healthy air. In 1844 she rented, from Lady Blatchford, Osborne House, overlooking the Solent, for a year's trial; she became so enchanted by the rural privacy of 'our island home' that the next year she purchased the house and estate for £26,000. 'It is impossible to imagine a prettier spot', she confided to her diary, thrilled with the trees, the sea and her private beach. 'And then we can walk about everywhere by ourselves without being followed or mobbed'.

Victoria knew that Osborne House would be too small for them all, and almost at once the Prince Consort laid the foundation stone of a new residence. It was designed by Thomas Cubitt in a Neapolitan style, with high towers and a first-floor loggia. Long before its completion in 1851, Albert had tackled the estate, laying out gardens and planting here England's first Christmas tree. His economies in running Buckingham Palace and the sale of Brighton Pavilion enabled them to spend £200,000 on furnishing the new house at Osborne, but it was all methodically done. Instead of buying a piano, the Prince hired one by the quarter. In the gardens he installed a Swiss cottage as a playroom where the boys could learn carpentry and their sisters cooking.

Immediately after the Prince Consort's death in 1861, Victoria left Windsor for the seclusion of Osborne. There, she told her children that the house must remain sacred to their father's memory. Nothing was to be changed – and nothing was changed until the Queen had herself died forty years later; the Prince Consort's walking-sticks were still being polished every day, and the inkstand on his writing-desk topped up; the pictures and ornaments he had liked were still in place. Victoria did make one addition, for at the entrance was built the

Durbar Room in 1891, reflecting her pride in the title 'Empress of India'. Indian craftsmen under Bhai Ram Singh decorated the interior with truly oriental splendour. Fittingly, it was at Osborne that the Queen died.

Since 1954, when the Queen first opened her great-great-grandmother's suite to the public, visitors have been able to see Victoria's dressing-table, with the toilet articles of Minton china and her writing-desk as she left them. The profusion of miniatures, paperweights, musical-boxes, fans, pincushions, statuettes and china dogs make an incomparable collection of Victoriana.

Because the Scottish Highlands touched a romantic chord in her heart, Victoria decided to rent Balmoral House, near Braemar, from the Fife Trustees in 1848. Prince Albert was just as enchanted, for it reminded him of his beloved Rosenau. 'The house is small but pretty', noted the Queen, and the country was 'wild and solitary, and yet cheerful and beautifully wooded'. By 1852, she had purchased the estate and begun to replace the house by a spacious granite residence; three years later the Royal Family moved into the new Balmoral, which looked from the outside like a great baronial castle, with a high tower, lesser turrets and gables. The inside was dominated by pitch pine and tartan, with particular tartans designed by herself and the Prince, and even tartan linoleum in the servants' rooms. All, she thought, was 'perfection' – furniture, wallpapers and floors.

The Queen became a model laird and a staunch supporter of the Braemar Gathering for the Highland games. As a widow, Victoria found an even greater seclusion here than at Osborne, spending perhaps five months of every twelve in the Highlands, which did not ease her Prime Minister's burdens: 'Carrying on the government of a country six hundred miles from the metropolis doubles the labour', bemoaned Disraeli. During the 1870s, she seemed content to let her ghillie, John Brown, with 'his warm heart and cheery way of saying things', rule the estate and much of the house. Brown became heartily detested by almost everyone else and on his accession, Edward VII personally ordered the profusion of cairns, monuments and garden seats to Brown's memory, donated by crowned heads, to be removed.

Although her aloofness earned her the name 'the Widow of Windsor', Victoria found the Castle too melancholy a place for prolonged stays, for she associated it with Albert's death. At neighbouring Frogmore she built an elaborate mausoleum for his remains, while the old Tudor chapel to the east of St. George's was lined with marble by Sir G. G. Scott and became the Albert Memorial Chapel.

The servants at Windsor never tired of talking of the visit of Napoleon III and the Empress Eugénie in happier days (one can still see the bed, with the French eagle at the foot, that they slept in during 1855). Nothing seemed to happen there in later years beyond the private command performances of children's choirs and colliery bands given in the Green Drawing Room. There are few Victorian remains in the Castle, for Queen Alexandra insisted on a thorough redecoration and, as a result, many *objets d'art* that her mother-in-law had collected were removed to Kensington and Osborne, while others were sold. It may still be possible for the collector to come across small items that had once formed part of Victoria's great hoard.

Victorian-Classical Furniture

Lindsay Boynton

A. C. Cooper

3

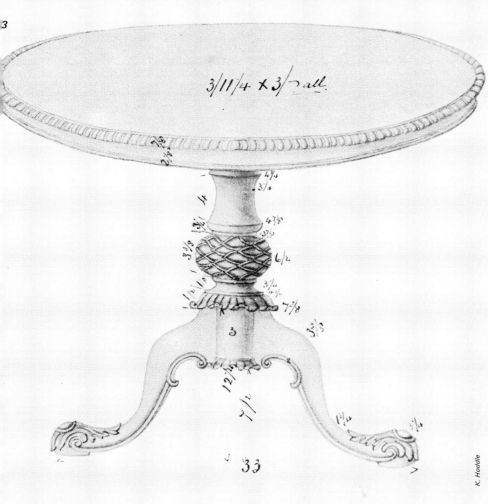

3/11/4 × 3/? all.

33

K. Hoddle

Fig. 1 **Table.** *This drawing-room table dates from about 1850. It has a mahogany stem and legs of the type illustrated in Figure 3, but with the unusual feature of an octagonal top just over forty inches across, with a burr veneer perhaps of maple, and a crossbanded and inlaid border of black, yellow and white. The top is a simpler version of the one designed by A. W. N. Pugin for Abney Hall, Cheshire, which is now in the Victoria and Albert Museum. (Private Collection, London.)*

Fig. 2 **Chair.** *Chairs are probably the commonest type of Victorian furniture to survive. Many of them are either upholstered armchairs or light, single chairs of the 'balloon-back' type, which seem to have been used throughout the house. This example, however, represents another type of more solid single chair of the mid-Victorian period. It appears somewhat awkward because it looks as if it ought to have a rail in the back, although it evidently never possessed one. On the other hand, the moulded cabriole legs, the finely figured mahogany top-rail and the elegantly sinuous curve (only partly visible in the illustration) of the vertical back-rails, all point to a good maker. He did in fact record his name in a trade label affixed to the underside of the seat: 'W. H. A. Roebuck, Cabinet-Maker, Upholsterer, Undertaker, & British-plate Glass dealer, 51, New Street, Huddersfield'. (Private Collection, London.)*

Fig. 3 **Design for a loo-table,** *Gillow of Lancaster. This type of table, with an oval or circular top on a centre support which splays into three legs, is descended from Regency tables and ultimately from the Georgian 'pillar and claw' table. It was intended originally for the game of loo, although obviously it lent itself to various other uses. The type was common throughout the Victorian period, especially in the middle of the century, and varied widely in quality. The top was often of well-figured walnut. This drawing is of particular interest because it is dated (1849) and was to be made in satinwood at a cost to the firm of £14.16s.2d.*

The massive, ornate and beautifully made 'Victorian-classical' furniture evolved from classical types of the eighteenth century and achieved its own distinctive style and charm

Two things are as obvious about Victorian furniture as they are about Victorian architecture: there is a lot of it and it is, or seems to be, far more varied in style than Georgian furniture. There is a lot of it because, compared with their Georgian predecessors, Victorian cabinet-makers had a large and expanding market based on a rapidly growing population and a general, if intermittent, rise in the standard of living; besides, the general standard of craftsmanship was higher in the nineteenth century and the furniture lasts well.

If nineteenth-century styles seem more complex than those of the eighteenth century, the reason is no doubt partly due to the capitulation of the civilised but limited artistic taste of the Georgian governing class before the non-taste of Victorian *nouveaux riches*, and partly due to the repeated battles between retrospective revivalists (who resurrected forms of Elizabethan, gothic, Louis XIV and other styles), and reformers who were out to purge furniture of its debased form and ornament and to substitute such styles as modern gothic, Arts and Crafts and Anglo-Japanese.

These Victorian styles, as well as the extreme prestigious designs produced for exhibitions, are generally easily recognised and have been extensively discussed and illustrated. A considerable proportion of such furniture is now in permanent public or private collections, and a great deal of it is excessively rare, large, ugly or otherwise undesirable for the general collector.

Solidly made, handsome furniture which avoided stylistic extremes

The vast output of Victorian furniture really has two main categories. One is the cheap and shoddy products of East End sweated labour, which supplied dealers all over the country; most of this has by now probably fallen to pieces. The other is the solidly made and often handsome furniture which thousands of conservatively minded middle and upper-middle class people bought, and which is the main concern of this article; the only difficulty is to give a name to it, since it avoids those stylistic extremes which are easily labelled.

The late Charles Handley-Read, acknowledging that the conservative mid-Victorian style eludes easy description, proposed a 'nameless' category. In a period when names of styles and types abound, this suggestion has its attractions; but we do need a name. Some of the post-Regency furniture has been called 'Sub-classical'; it is justifiable to call the furniture described here 'Victorian-classical'. It descends, after all, from classical types evolved in the eighteenth century, yet it is recognisably Victorian and not pastiche or reproduction. It has one disadvantage from the present-day collector's standpoint, which indeed it shares with much genuine Georgian furniture: its size. To remark that houses and rooms were spacious and their furniture correspondingly large is to state the obvious, but it needs to be repeated; much occasional furniture which purports to be Georgian never saw the eighteenth century. Because much genuine 'Victorian-classical' furniture is also large, the process of destruction has already begun, indeed has been going on for some time.

Victorian-classical furniture combined fine quality wood and excellent workmanship

'Victorian-classical' furniture was made for doctors, clergymen, gentlemen and others who wanted new, but not eccentrically or aggressively modern, furniture, which would look well in their comfortable houses and stand up to wear and tear from their large families rather more successfully, perhaps, than some of the flimsily elegant, late Georgian products. As such households gave way to smaller family units, a good deal of their furniture must have been sold and often broken up.

Subsequent to the vogue, this furniture was regarded as almost unsaleable. Happily, larger houses are now returning to favour and there is hope therefore that the best of the remaining Victorian-classical furniture will be saved. It does, after all, have distinct advantages. It has never been faked or reproduced and, given the large quantities of fine wood involved, it is not likely to be. It is almost invariably of excellent quality and usually in a good state of preservation. Because of its size, it is still relatively cheap. Not every piece is handsome but many are.

The relatively unexplored field which this sort of furniture offers is emphasised by the fact that none of these illustrations has been reproduced before. Furthermore, such furniture is mostly still within the reach of the average collector.

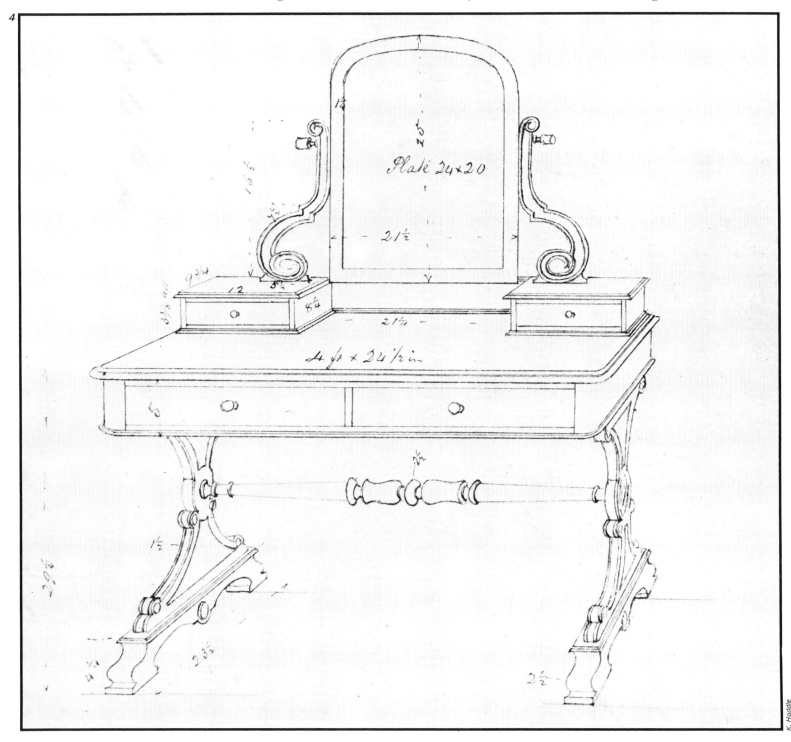

Fig. 4 **Dressing-table design**, *Gillow of Lancaster. Like the Curwen Wardrobe (Fig. 9), this design is dated 1865 and was to be made in birchwood. Its cost to the firm was £8.14s.5¾d. Dressing-tables of this type are still to be found easily and cheaply. With their swing mirrors, rows of drawers and rococo legs, they are particularly evocative of the mid-Victorian period. They are usually well made, generally of mahogany.*

Fig. 5 **Dressing-table**, *Constantine. This dressing-table, of finely figured walnut, was made by a prominent Leeds firm, Constantine and Co., active from the 1820s to the 1880s. All its known furniture is of excellent quality. A writing-table, armchair, dressing-glass, hat-stand and stool by this firm, from the collection at Broughton Hall, Yorkshire, were exhibited at Temple Newsam House, Leeds, in 1971. The identification of this dressing-table is from the firm's trade label which is pasted underneath the drawers, with the number 24536 and the workman's name: Lassey. This degree of detail is not found on Georgian trade labels. The date of this piece (height to top of mirror 5 feet 6 inches by 3 feet 10½ inches by 23 inches deep) is about 1850–1860. Its style, particularly in the stand and stretchers, is reminiscent of Regency forms, but the effect of the whole is an excellent example of 'Victorian-classical'.*
(Private Collection, London.)

Fig. 7 **Wardrobe.** *This piece represents the best of 'Victorian-classical' in its good proportions (height 6 feet 9 inches, width 4 feet 8 inches, depth 21½ inches) and markedly restrained use of carved ornament and a few simple mouldings on the doors and cornice. It is beautifully made, and the illustration shows the finely finished mahogany drawers and trays on the left-hand side; the right-hand side provides plenty of hanging-space. The maker is not known in this case, but the general appearance and the flush-fitting brass handles inside are similar to Gillow designs of the middle of the century. (Private Collection, London.)*

Fig. 6 **Cabinet**, *Gillow of Lancaster. This cabinet dates from about 1890. It measures 4 feet 4 inches high by 4 feet 2 inches wide by 16 inches deep, and is stamped 'GILLOWS 16649' inside the centre cupboard. The carcase is of oak, with inlay of various light woods and mother of pearl. It complements the design in Figure 11 very nicely, for its proportions and general form are partly derived from Sheraton designs. The marquetry, however, owes at least as much to the sixteenth-century Renaissance as it does to the late eighteenth century. It is thus very far from being a pastiche; the total effect is distinctly late Victorian. (Private Collection, Buckinghamshire.)*

Fig. 8 *Osborne House, Isle of Wight,* the State Drawing-Room. Although it fulfilled the function of a State-room for the reception of important visitors who made their way to the Queen's Court when it was in the Isle of Wight, the scale and furnishings of this drawing-room are modest compared with similar rooms at Buckingham Palace or Windsor Castle. As Mr. Edward Joy pointed out, in his article on the furniture at Osborne, all of it has been specifically designed for comfort. He has identified much of it as the work of the outstanding firm of Holland & Sons between 1845 and 1850. The furniture in this room, with its handsome armchairs, sofas and circular and rectangular tables, bears a strong resemblance to Regency models.

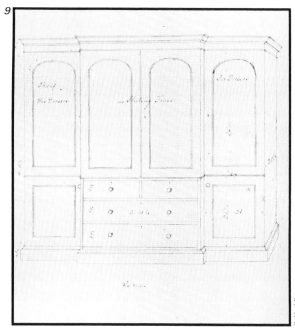

Fig. 9 *Design for a wardrobe,* Gillow of Lancaster. This design, dated 1865, is described as a 'Curwen Wardrobe' in the firm's books, probably after a customer; as an example of a genuine contemporary name applied to furniture which has Georgian precedents, it contrasts with the frequent adoption, in the nineteenth century, of fancy names such as 'monks' bench'. This wardrobe was to be executed in birch, a wood not much used in the Georgian period but quite common in Victorian furniture, particularly in pieces intended for the bedroom. Similar wardrobes are still fairly common. They are usually very well made and designed, with a combination of drawers, trays and hanging-space, which is useful today, whereas the Georgian 'gentleman's press',,with trays alone, is less acceptable.

Fig. 10 **Chest of drawers.** The Georgian ancestry of this type of furniture is apparent, but there are significant differences. Victorian cabinet-makers seem to have preferred flat fronts to curved fronts for chests, and they habitually used turned wooden handles of the type developed during the Regency period rather than brass mounts. A feature of this example (height 3 feet 8 inches, width 3 feet 9 inches, depth $21\frac{1}{2}$ inches) is that the plinth is joined to the bottom drawer and moves with it, as the illustration shows; this construction is found elsewhere on nineteenth-century drawer furniture, but not on eighteenth-century pieces. The graded size of the drawers, on the other hand, is a direct continuation of Georgian practice, although the mouldings on their edges are much bolder than Georgian cock-beading. The drawers are made of mahogany with the finest possible dovetails; the front is veneered with burr walnut. The special interest of this piece lies in its being stamped on the top left-hand drawer with the maker's name: 'James Winter & Sons, 101, Wardour St., Soho, London'. It has often been stated that signed, stamped or labelled Victorian furniture is exceptional, but there is in fact a great deal so identified, and it is much commoner than with Georgian examples. This adds interest, of course, to the collecting of Victorian furniture. (*Private Collection, London.*)

Fig. 11 **Cabinet design,** Gillow of Lancaster. This sketch is dated 1882, and thus extends this selection of Gillow designs to the late Victorian period. Its particular interest lies in its Sheraton flavour; the revival of interest in Chippendale designs dates from the 1830s, but it was in the 1870s and thereafter that Victorian furniture-designers turned again to the late eighteenth-century elegance which was so much in keeping with contemporary notions about light rooms and furniture.

VICTORIAN NURSERY LIFE

Juliet Smith

"DEAR, DEAR; *what* IT IS TO BE A MOTHER OF A FAMILY, AND *all* OF... ..."JUST THE IMAGE OF HI... DEAR PA." THEM SICK"

...INKIN... ...GOES WHEN THEY DIE... NOW GER...LINE MAUD... ...TTEN D T... ...HAVE ANY *stuff* ABOUT MA...RYING FOR LOVE. IT DOESN'T...AT...E ABOUT ELIZA; SHE'S GOING ...SEE THE "Wax Cry"

Fig. 1 (Frontispiece) **Nursery screen,** *English, late nineteenth century. Wood, canvas and paper collage. Nursery draughts were excluded by folding screens which were decorated with brightly coloured scraps. (Mary Hillier Collection.)*

Fig. 2 **Mother and child** *by Frederick George Stephens, 1854. Oil on canvas. Victorian mothers tended to have a distant and slightly unreal relationship with their children. Nurses carried out the day-to-day business of upbringing, while the mothers were awesome creatures who appeared infrequently in the nursery and were idolised. (Tate Gallery, London.)*

Fig. 3 **Good morning** *from* At Home *illustrated by J. G. Sowerby and decorated by Thomas Crane. Many Victorian children's books give a clear, if somewhat sweetened, view of nursery life. The night nursery, seen here, was often an austere, unheated room providing very few physical comforts.*

Fig. 4 **One O'Clock P.M: The Nursery Dinner** *by F. Craxton, from the* Illustrated Times, *1864. Engraving. Family life in the Victorian nursery was not always as rosy as most pictures would have one believe. Despite the severe restraints imposed on children, they somehow survived.*

A safe little world enclosed behind bars, the Victorian nursery could be a cosy place of security or a cold, harsh prison of childhood

The lamplighter is passing slowly down the street. At a window high above, children's faces are pressed to the glass as they watch this familiar sight. The glass is crossed by iron bars – 'how the children disliked these bars'. Marks of little teeth were plainly discernible along them, and no prisoners could have tried more perseveringly to shake them from their sockets.

In the memoirs and children's books of the Victorian period, the children somehow seem to be spectators of the adult world rather than participators. They watch the lamplighter and the crossing-sweeper and the organ-grinder. They get to know the ordinary passers-by and invent exotic stories about them. They sit on the stairs and watch, this time through the bars of the banisters, as the richly dressed ladies and gentlemen pass through the hall on their way in to dinner.

Perhaps it is not fanciful to think of these children as always behind bars, for they were confined to a world of their own – the world of the nursery. Even the fondest mother would have thought it extraordinary to wish to bath her own baby, or brush her daughter's hair, and some parents saw very little of their children who none the less adored them from a distance. We can read of this in memoirs such as Churchill's *My Early Life*, and in many children's books. In *Odd*, for instance, Mrs. Stuart saw as little of her children as her husband did; 'her time was fully occupied in attending committee meetings, opening bazaars, and superintending numerous pet projects for en-

nobling and raising the standard of morality among the masses'. Mothers would pay short and sometimes alarming visits to the nursery and arouse the same feelings of half-fearful excitement as when one of the gods descended from Olympus to visit the mortals.

The nursery had its own hierarchy – nurse, under-nurse and nursery maid in the grander establishments – and its own laws, as inflexible as those of the Medes and Persians. It was an autocracy, and, as in all autocracies, the happiness of the subjects depended on the character of the autocrat. With a kind nurse it could be a very happy life; with a cruel one, it could be wretched.

Fortunately, there are many more records of good nurses than bad ones. They were usually known as 'Nursey' – not 'Nanny' at that date – or sometimes by their surnames: 'Just Dawson, my Lord, neither Miss nor Missis, bless your little heart', as Lord Fauntleroy's new nurse explained to her punctilious charge. Nursey sat in a rocking-chair and wore 'a sober stuff dress'. Sometimes she crackled in a huge starched apron, and children slipped off her lap. She had a cap with streamers and an inexhaustible fund of stories, mostly about her previous charges. There were also tales of a cautionary nature about children who came to an untimely end through playing with matches or eating tempting red berries.

The nurse was not only law-maker and judge, but also executioner. Punishments ranged from 'a good whipping' to solitary confinement with a text to learn. Users of bad language had their mouths washed out with soap. A box on the ear was much in vogue as a quick, on-the-spot form of retribution, and, as a result, some children's hearing was impaired for life.

Within the nursery, children would see a room lit only by firelight, for on a winter's afternoon the lamps would not be brought in until teatime at five o'clock. The battered old nursery table, with the baby's high wooden chair drawn up, would be ready laid with mugs for the children's milk and a heavy brown teapot with a patchwork cosy for Nurse. Perhaps one of those exquisite dolls' tea-sets would be laid out on a little table by the fire, just far enough away for the wax faces of Florinda, Emily and Clarice, seated stiffly around it, to be safe from melting. There were various kinds of tea-sets, ranging from 'white china with a green rim, big enough to make real tea in', through 'tin tea-sets where the lids would come off' to 'wooden ones, where they were stuck on'.

In one corner of the room the big dolls' house would stand, in another, the old rocking-horse, his dappled flanks scarred by generations of drumming heels. The draught from the door would be shut out by a folding screen, covered with brightly coloured scraps: children with kittens, the Queen with the infant Prince of Wales, posies of heartsease. Other pictures would hang on the walls, their subjects falling into three main categories – the heroic, the religious and the whimsical. The first might be represented by Lady Butler's tragic Crimean scene, *The Roll Call*, the second by Sant's *The Infant Samuel* and the third by one of those embarrassing pictures of pink-cheeked, golden-haired children dressing up (*Borrowed Plumes*), or skating (*Will it Bear?*), or hard at work (*Ironing for Dolly*).

In that twilight hour before tea, when it was too

5

6

7

dark to read, the children would sit around the great cage-like nursery fire-guard (much in demand for games of Zoos or Prisoners) and tell stories. Later, they would be dressed up and brought downstairs to join their parents at dessert. As a character in one of Mrs. Ewing's books observes: 'I like to see children come in to dessert, when they have good manners; besides, it keeps the nurses up to their work'.

The night nursery was often a Spartan apartment, with fires only allowed in time of illness, or, in more indulgent households, for the morning bath, which was brought in and set down by the hearth. The hot water came in a jug with the towel folded over the top to keep the towel warm and the water hot. Dressing usually required a certain amount of help from Nurse, owing to the complexity of children's clothes which fastened at the most inaccessible places. It is impossible to generalise about clothes over the whole Victorian period, but they shared certain properties. Girls wore a great many layers of underclothes and petticoats, which made dressing and undressing a lengthy process. Boys were liable to be the victims of their mother's romantic fantasies, and had to appear in company in a kind of fancy dress, as sailor boys, romantic Highlanders or miniature Cavaliers: 'A graceful childish figure in a black velvet suit with a lace collar, and with lovelocks waving about the handsome, manly little face'. It was hard luck.

Hats were compulsory in all weathers

Even in the country, comfort was a secondary consideration. It is true that dresses could be protected by 'large holland overalls', but hats were compulsory for both boys and girls, to shield them from cold in winter and heat in summer. We read of one eight-year-old girl at the end of the century, going out to tea with a country neighbour attired in 'a stiff white frock and tan shoes and stockings, with her large white leghorn hat and feathers and little white silk gloves'.

Once dressed, there was nursery breakfast, not a very inspiring meal. Gwen Raverat describes it in her picture of a Victorian childhood, *Period Piece*: 'We had porridge for breakfast, with salt, not sugar, and milk to drink . . . It is true that twice a week we had, at the end of breakfast, one piece of toast, spread with a thin layer of that dangerous luxury, jam. But of course, not butter too. Butter and jam on the same bit of bread would have been an unheard-of indulgence – a disgraceful orgy'

After family prayers, there would be the morning walk, accompanied by Nurse, wheeling the youngest member of the family in the baby carriage. One can still see various models in museums. Most seem to have been narrow, allowing only for the slimmest baby, with iron wheels and a wooden handle fore and aft. The smarter versions were in basket-work, and some, for slightly older children, were pushed from behind. These were made like real carriages, with a wooden horse in front which moved up and down as the wheels turned, while the passenger lashed out with a small leather whip.

In the country, of course, children had much more freedom, and played by themselves out of doors. One odd feature of Victorian life was that parents seemed to scorn the perils of drowning.

Fig. 5 **Nursery games.** *Victorian engraving.*

Fig. 6 **A Soft Answer** *by George du Maurier, 1889. The caption reads:* 'Jane, I saw that Policeman speak to you. That's the Third Policeman I've seen you speaking to this Morning. I can't allow that!' 'No, Ma'am. But the Policemen always do admire Baby so – they can't 'elp stoppin' and askin' about 'im. They all say as they never see such a fine Child!'

Fig. 7 **I was conducted to the nursery door** *by Densdale from Girls' Own Paper, 1885. Engraving.*

K. Hoddle

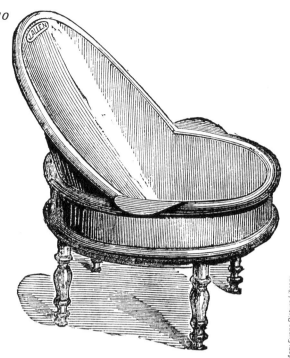

Mary Evans Picture Library

Fig. 8 **Nursery** *in Miss Miles' dolls' house, c.1870. (Bethnal Green Museum, London.)*

Fig. 9 **Victorian nursery objects.** Clockwise: *Mug and plate, possibly Swansea, early nineteenth century; Staffordshire money-box with transfer-printed Indian sports; Staffordshire potty; jar for louse ointment, used on Friday evenings after washing, late nineteenth century; feeding-bottle, possibly Spode, c.1830; rattle, probably not English. (Private Collection.)*

Fig. 10 **Nursery- and hip-bath combined,** *Victorian.*

Again and again, one reads of small children, quite unable to swim, being allowed to play by rivers or lakes, with punts, canoes and home-made rafts.

In the afternoon, there was always the danger of being taken by one's mother on a series of boring calls, or sent with a nourishing broth to the cottage of a long-retired, bed-ridden retainer.

With no wireless or television, and comparatively few treats and outings, Victorian children had a lot of time on their hands. In spite of the rich variety of toys made at that date, they spent a very high proportion of their time playing imaginative and acting games: 'niggers and tomtoms and going Fantee', for instance. Their reading was a strange mixture of precocity and childishness. They seem to have been familiar with an astonishing number of the classics by the age of ten or eleven, yet saw nothing odd in continuing to take *Little Folks* magazine until the age of seventeen. They were much given to word games – acrostics, metagrams, riddle-me-rees and transposition puzzles. In the Golden Jubilee competition of *Little Folks*, Louisa Reith, aged eight, derived eight hundred and eighty-three words from the letters QUEEN VICTORIA. On Sundays, when small children's play was confined to the Noah's Ark, these puzzles gave way to the dreaded Bible Exercises, and the poor little folk wrestled with problems like 'Where are little children told to keep themselves from idols?' and 'Who is the only woman spoken of in the Bible as a sister-in-law?'

Children were also infected by the general Victorian passion for handicrafts. Their samplers show what high standards were expected of them, and they were expert at producing a useful article for the Christmas Bazaar – 'a dainty brush and comb bag, made of a square of Madras muslin put over a similar piece of electric-blue sateen', or 'some large Zulu hats, ingeniously adapted to form flower baskets'.

The world of the Victorian nursery has gone for ever, but we can still appreciate its atmosphere through the toys and books, the pictures and puzzles, and all the other memories it has left behind, as rich and as varied as the scraps on one of its own screens.

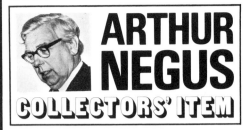

ARTHUR NEGUS COLLECTORS' ITEM

CHRISTMAS CARDS

As today, no Victorian or Edwardian Christmas was complete without a colourful display of cards. However, our ancestors devoted more attention to this integral part of the Christmas festivities than we do. Each card was carefully chosen in the knowledge that when it reached that large Victorian mantelpiece at the other end, it would be subject to some study, and, possibly, to some criticism. Luckily for today's collector, the best cards would be preserved in the family album. These albums are beginning to be seen in their proper light as the unique records of changing attitudes to many subjects.

The notion of sending a pictorial greetings card at Christmas must be credited to Henry Cole, the first director of the Victoria and Albert Museum, and since the results of new printing techniques could be cheaply obtained by nearly everyone, the idea soon became fashionable.

Cole's card, produced in 1843, was a picture of a family Christmas dinner, but many of its successors were little more than pictorial visiting-cards. Commercial printers, already experienced in producing Valentines, illustrated writing-paper and religious text cards, had no difficulty in stimulating public enthusiasm for these Christmas novelties. Each year there would be a new gimmick in the shops, such as a complicated folding card, a padded scented card, a mechanical card, or an embossed card with perforated edges, as each manufacturer competed for the market. The advent of the postcard in Great Britain in 1870, and in the United States in 1873, greatly increased the demand, since cards could now be sent for a halfpenny instead of a penny. Many of the most interesting examples of Christmas card art exist on postcards, especially during the Edwardian period when photographs became popular components of Christmas card design. Our taste in matters of design may not coincide with that of the Victorians, but

their Christmas cards remain to show that in typographic inventiveness and technical daring they have few equals.

Collecting Hints

The Victorians usually sorted their cards according to subject matter, and there is no reason why today's collector should not do likewise. There is no lack of choice, especially among Christmas subjects. Such a collection, embracing cards up to, say, the 1920s, becomes a graphic record of ever-changing popular taste, and of ephemeral fashions, such as the Japanese craze of the 1880s. Then there are cards designed specially for children, comic cards and military cards (the First World War produced many fascinating examples). There are animated or novelty cards. There have even been gramophone records on cards! Religious cards, royalty on cards, political Christmas cards — the list is endless. An alternative idea is to study the cards of a particular artist, or even the output of one manufacturer. For example, many of the Christmas cards designed for children were drawn by well-known illustrators of children's books and magazines.

Where To Buy

Antique markets and the less expensive antique shops are the collector's main source.

Prices

Early complicated novelty cards are already worth pounds rather than shillings. Victorian albums of stuck-down cards (often combined with newspaper cuttings, poetry, scraps, etc.),

are becoming increasingly expensive at a few pounds each. And certain artists, such as Kate Greenaway and Aubrey Beardsley, are naturally very hard to come by. Yet accumulations of cards in reasonable condition can still be found for a few pence.

Above *Thoughts,* a late Victorian Christmas card with embossed greeting and flowers.

Opposite: *'Cheero!' To Blighty and You,* a World War I divisional Christmas card.

Right *A Happy Christmas,* an Edwardian commercial hand-painted postcard bearing a seasonal verse.

Bottom left *With loving Christmas Greetings,* an Edwardian children's card dated 1903.

Bottom right *Best Wishes,* a World War I embroidered card. The front flap forms a pocket which holds a small greetings card.

BOARD & TABLE GAMES

Robert Bell

Nursery games of the last century were intended to amuse and instruct, as, indeed, is still the intention to this day

Games played a far larger role in family life before television and the wireless provided professional entertainment in the home at the turn of a switch. Many Victorian bygones of the nursery and the drawing-room survive – silent reminders of a way of life that has become history.

Figure 8 shows a box of building-bricks, which doubled up as a puzzle, each face carrying part of a different picture. One picture was reproduced on the front of the box and five others were shown inside. Music is represented by a fiddle and trumpet; there is a shop counter, a jack-in-the-box, a ball, a mechanical drummer, a stove with kettle and pans, and a jelly-mould, the last now a collector's piece; a doll in a bath, Punch in a jester's costume, a whistling top, a rocking-horse, a doll and a box of building-bricks. Other brightly coloured pictures show fruit, nuts and vegetables; two sheets are devoted to flowers, and the last to articles found in the carpentry shed, garden and dairy.

The acrobats in Figure 4 have suffered considerable injuries in the course of their long and dangerous career. The original advertisement ran: 'Crandall's Great Show of Acrobats exhibited at the house of the purchaser every afternoon and evening with no postponement on account of weather. Matinée every morning. Admission free, and children half price'.

These ingenious pieces are made of wood, and locked together with parallel saw-cuts. The two sides of the body are dressed in different circus costume, thus doubling the possible variations.

Nursery amusements were frequently linked with the acquisition of knowledge. Happy Family games permitted the grouping of related objects. Examples are the orders of architecture; national costumes, flags, capital cities and rulers; historical episodes with places and personalities; highlights in

Fig. 1 **Box for the repulsion-bell,** *a variation of the teetotum which gave a score. Dice were never used at this early date. (Mary Hillier Collection.)*

Fig. 2 **Victorian jigsaw or 'dissected' puzzle** *and its box,* c.1860. *The puzzle is entitled 'My Birthday Presents'. (Hannas Collection.)*

Fig. 3 **Wooden Pope Joan board** *with counters and cards. The cards have no numbers, and the pips all point in the same direction. (Author's Collection.)*

Fig. 4 **Crandall's Acrobats,** *an American wooden building game. (Author's Collection.)*

Fig. 5 **Cards and equipment** *for* Bell and Hammer, *played at least as early as 1816. The dice are marked on one face only. (Author's Collection.)*

Fig. 6 **Victorian children** *playing with alphabet blocks. Engraving by Charles Weeks.*

the history of science; and the counties of England.

The Travellers, or A Tour Through Europe (Fig. 9), published by William Spooner in December 1842, is representative of a considerable number of educational race games. An aquatint of Europe is shown with each country filled in with perspective views of its capital and important cities or ports. The five travellers start from points marked 'S' at the bottom of the map on longitude and latitude intersections, and make their way north, south, east or west, as directed by the spins of a teetotum, paying or receiving counters when landing on marked intersections. The finishing-points are Vienna, St. Petersburg, Stockholm, Berlin and London.

The little pictures in these games are worth studying with a hand-lens; in this one, the contemporary shipping includes a screw-barque, and a whale has tossed a long-boat into the air with its tail; there is also an extraordinary chariot dashing over the Russian steppes.

The Game of the Race (Fig. 13) simulated a steeplechase. The moves of the horses were controlled by the throw of a cubic die, and on certain spaces penalties were inflicted. At eleven, the horse refused to jump a gate; at twenty-four, it was trapped by the incoming tide; at thirty-eight, it lost its way; at fifty-four, it threw its rider; at sixty-seven, it broke its leg; and at eighty-eight, it baulked at a hedge. The owner of the first horse to reach one hundred won the game. The little lead horses from this game are of considerable interest to followers of the Turf, the jockeys being dressed in the racing-colours of famous owners of the day.

Bell and Hammer (Fig. 5) came from Germany, and was played in England at least as early as 1816 and therefore is not strictly a Victorian game. It was still being played as late as 1870, but had vanished by the turn of the century.

Eight dice were used, each with five plain surfaces; the sixth sides are marked with the numbers 1 to 6, a bell or a hammer. There were five picture cards: an Inn, a White Horse, a Hammer, a Bell and a Bell and Hammer. A dicing-cup and an auctioneer's gavel completed the set.

Halma (Fig. 12) was invented in about 1880. In

7

PRINCE ALBERT *of* SAXE COBOURG

THE HUSBAND ELECT OF QUEEN VIC...

PRINCE ALBERT
OF SAXE COBOURG AND GOTHA,
The Husband-elect of Queen Victoria.

9

10

8

the two-handed form each player had nineteen men arranged in his own 'camp', the walls being marked by a double line. Only one man may be moved in any turn of play, either as a single step in any direction on to an adjacent empty square, or by leaping over a man, or men, in any direction on to an empty square immediately beyond. The first player to occupy all the squares in the enemy camp is the winner.

Asalto, or *Officers and Sepoys* (Fig. 10), is a late form of *Fox and Geese*. The pieces move along the marked lines orthogonally or diagonally. The green boundary represents a fort, and one player places two red marbles (officers) in any two holes within its walls. His opponent places twenty-four green marbles (sepoys) in the holes in the surrounding countryside. All pieces move one hole along any marked line, but the sepoys must always move towards the fort. The officers capture by a short leap, and are 'huffed' if they fail to make a possible capture. The sepoys are unable to jump, but win if they occupy every hole in the fort, or if they immobilise the officers. If they become too few to accomplish these objectives, the officers are victorious. The game received its alternative

Fig. 7 *Prince Albert jigsaw puzzle*, *English*, *c.1839. Issued shortly before Queen Victoria's wedding on 10 February, 1840, this is a very early jigsaw puzzle. (Author's Collection.)*

Fig. 8 *Victorian building-bricks. These bricks doubled as a puzzle, each face carrying part of a different picture. (Author's Collection.)*

Fig. 9 *The Travellers, or A Tour Through Europe, 1842. (There was a second edition in 1852.) This instructional game was made of twelve sections mounted on linen, and was played with dice or a teetotum and gaming counters. (Author's Collection.)*

name from the mutiny in Bengal in 1857. The same board can be used for *Solitaire*.

Ludo (Fig. 11) was introduced into England and patented in about 1896 as a modification of the national game of India, *Pacheesi* or *Pachisi*. One of the Mogul emperors, Akbar (1542–1605), played it in the courtyard at Agra on a board of inlaid marble. In the centre was a dais four feet high on which he and his courtiers sat, while sixteen slave girls from the harem, wearing dresses of different colours, moved about the red and white squares as directed by the throws of cowrie shells. Traces of these royal boards are still visible at Agra and Allahabad. The board in Figure 11 was used for *Ludo* and *Royal Ludo*; the latter is a variant which serves to date this board as an early one.

Pope Joan was a game for any number of players, each starting with thirty counters. A fifty-two-card pack was used with the eight of diamonds removed, and a revolving circular tray (Fig. 3) divided into eight compartments labelled: Pope, Matrimony, Intrigue, Ace, King, Queen, Knave and Game.

These are some of the table games that amused

and instructed Victorian children. Many of them have been brought up to date; but even those that have been forgotten, when brought to light, can still amuse and instruct.

MUSEUMS AND COLLECTIONS
Victorian table and board games may be seen at the following:
GREAT BRITAIN
Edinburgh: Museum of Childhood
London: Victoria and Albert Museum
Oxford: Pitt Rivers Museum
York: Castle Museum

FURTHER READING
Board and Table Games from Many Civilizations by R. C. Bell, Vols. I and II, London, 1960–69.
Table Games of Georgian and Victorian Days by F. B. R. Whitehouse, London, 1951.
The Handbook of Games by William Pole et al., Vol. I, London, 1890.

Fig. 10 *Asalto board*, *c.1860. The contemporary glass marbles, which vary in size, are not true spheres and contain flecks of metal. (Author's Collection.)*

Fig. 11 *Board for Ludo and Royal Ludo*, *c.1900. The men are of turned wood. (Author's Collection.)*

Fig. 12 *Halma board*, *c.1890. Wood with bone pegs. The players attempted to occupy the entire enemy camp by moving or leaping their pegs. (Author's Collection.)*

Fig. 13 *The Game of the Race*, *c.1850. Note the lead horses and riders and the dice, cups and dice-box which are also Victorian. (Author's Collection.)*

Percy Muir

THE BOOKS OF CRANE, CALDECOTT & GREENAWAY

The introduction of commercial colour-printing-presses allowed the publication of attractive children's books on mainly traditional subjects

In 1864 or '65, just over thirty years after George Baxter had patented the first commercially viable process of printing in colour, Edmund Evans, a London wood-engraver, commissioned Walter Crane (1845–1915) to design toy-books for a sixpenny series to be published by George Routledge. The books consisted of eight pages and only three colours could be afforded; tinted paper was used to provide an illusion of extra colour. To assure even a bare margin of profit a run of ten thousand was needed.

These toy-books sold like hot cakes and made Crane's reputation. He was not yet twenty-one when he began the series, and comparatively unknown; eleven years later, when his last title appeared, he was probably the most popular illustrator of his day. As to his talent as a designer, the various purposes to which he applied it would make a list of well nigh every article of household decoration' (Dictionary of National Biography).

There were thirty-eight Crane toy-books, the majority costing sixpence, but a handful of the later titles cost one shilling. The subjects were mostly traditional: A.B.Cs, nursery rhymes and fairy-tales, with an occasional, but not always successful, venture into more original fields.

The first two titles were The Railroad Alphabet and The Farmyard Alphabet, the latter with the animals dressed up, inevitably, as humans. The Multiplication Table in Verse is not at all dull; 'Twice Five', for example, has a particularly attractive picture of ten steamboats anchored in Plymouth Sound, although it is hardly typical of the artist.

King Luckieboy's Party is full of fun.

In 1877, however, Crane and Evans surpasse all these with The Baby's Opera, followed by Th Baby's Bouquet (1878) and The Baby's Own Aeso (1887), which are among their best productions Much more substantial than the toy-books, con taining fifty-six pages in picture-board covers an selling at five shillings each, they gave both artis and printer more scope; and both exploited it to th full. Despite the price, they, like the toy-books sold in tens of thousands.

By 1875 Crane had already flirted with anothe publisher of colour-books, Marcus Ward, and ha produced for him an amusing booklet for adults printed entirely in brown, Mrs. Mundi at Home; i 1885, with Slate and Pencilvania, he began work o a more lucrative series of toy-books published b Ward at half-a-crown. They were not printed b Evans; the illustrations were produced litho graphically, giving results which were more garis than those produced by the xylographic process.

Crane extended his activities as a book-illustrato although not always to his own advantage. H joined William Morris' Socialist League in 188 and contributed pastoral head-pieces to Morris socialist tracts. He also designed the wrapper fo Fabian Essays.

Evans did not easily find a successor to Crane It is almost impossible to date the toy-book accurately, but Crane does not seem to have pro duced any after 1876, and only one of them can b attributed with any confidence to that year. Ther was a gap until 1878, when the Christmas seaso saw the first of a new series.

These were the work of Randolph Caldecot (1846–86), a young man who had started his work ing life as a bank clerk in Cheshire, and had broke off in 1872 at the age of twenty-six to work i London as an artist.

He was befriended by Henry Blackburn, th editor of London Society, and it is said that it wa

TOMMY was a silly boy,
  "I can fly," he said ;
He started off, but very soon
  He tumbled on his head.

His little sister Prue was there,
  To see how he would do it ;
She knew that, after all his boast,
  Full dearly Tom would rue it !

K. Hoddle

A. C. Cooper

YE · GOOD · KING · ARTHVR

J. Freeman

Fig. 1 **Page from Under the Window,** *written and illustrated by Kate Greenaway (1846–1901), published by George Routledge and Sons, London, 1878. Proof. On a visit to Edmund Evans, the London wood-engraver, Kate Greenaway brought with her a collection of coloured drawings and verses. Evans seized upon them and the outcome,* Under the Window, *probably sold some 100,000 copies. (Borough of Camden Libraries and Arts Department.)*

Fig. 2 **Drawing for A frog he would a-wooing go,** *illustrated by Randolph Caldecott (1846–86) and published in 1883. Pen, ink and water-colour. One of Caldecott's series of picture-books, this shows his great talent and delicacy of touch. (Victoria and Albert Museum, London.)*

Fig. 3 **Ye Good King Arthur** *by Walter Crane (1845–1915). Pen, ink and water-colour drawing for a book-illustration. Although sometimes pretentious, Crane was probably the most popular illustrator of his day, and made innumerable drawings for every sort of book. (British Museum, London.)*

Caldecott's drawings for this journal that attracted J. D. Cooper, a wood-engraver who was looking for an artist to illustrate Washington Irving's *Old Christmas*. Caldecott was attracted by the idea, and during the year 1874 he completed over one hundred drawings for the book. Cooper engraved them to a high artistic standard, but it was not easy to find a publisher for the work of a comparatively unknown artist.

Macmillan finally issued the book towards the end of 1875; it was post-dated 1876, as was the custom. It was an immediate success and the reason according to Blackburn was that the author had been 'so closely followed – if not overtaken – by his illustrator'.

This book is not in colour; there is a tinted background to the title-page and to some of the full-page drawings, and the device is not altogether successful. It was not intended as a book for children and it was not printed by Evans, but by Clark of Edinburgh. Nevertheless, *Old Christmas* and its companion *Bracebridge Hall*, published the following year, are twin glories of Caldecott's brief career and cannot be passed over in any serious consideration of his book-illustrations.

Unlike Crane, Caldecott had received virtually

the earlier productions and the extended possibilities offered by the increase in price and demand, all combined to make the new series more appealing than the old. It is arguable, moreover, that Caldecott was a finer and less pretentious artist than Crane.

Each of the new series was to contain not only nine pages in full colour, including the pictorial cover, but also at least twenty line-drawings to be printed in the text. Caldecott was instructed to make all the drawings in black and white, and, for those to be printed in colour, key-proofs would be provided, printed in brown ink, the tint also used for the letter-press (Fig. 6). Caldecott would then colour the proof, bearing in mind that Evans would use a maximum of five specified colours in the finished article. A colour proof would then be submitted for the artist's approval.

The results were little short of incredible. An effect was produced that eludes all but the most elaborate of modern colour-processes. As to the lasting qualities of the boxwood blocks, it is enough to say that after taking hundreds of thousands of impressions from them, they show little, if any, deterioration today.

Caldecott's first bank appointment was at Whitchurch in Shropshire, then, as now, a small country

Fig. 4 **Drawing for John Gilpin,** *illustrated by Randolph Caldecott. Pen, ink and water-colour. Caldecott's bucolic experiences in Shropshire had a profound influence on his work. A large number of his books were about horses and the countryside, and it is typical that in this illustration of John Gilpin riding to Edmonton the horse shares the centre of the picture with his unfortunate rider. (Victoria and Albert Museum.)*

no artistic training. He had not learned to draw on wood and any of his work that was not reproduced by mechanical process was photographed on wood for the engraver to work on. At the time of Evans' approach to him he was primarily a black-and-white artist. It needed courage and foresight on Evans' part to entrust a whole new series of toy-books to such a novice, and it is clear from the rather vague details in Evans' reminiscences that the artist had to be gently coaxed through the successive stages of reproduction. Thus, even more than with Crane, Evans must be given a lion's share of the credit for the ensuing success.

This, together with the experience gained from

town. He doubtless had an allowance from his father, a well-to-do accountant in Chester, which enabled him to lodge in a comfortable farmhouse and to jog around the countryside in his leisure hours in a gig, occasionally attending the meets of the local hunt.

These bucolic experiences profoundly influenced his work as an artist for he was at his best when depicting rural scenes. It is characteristic that one of his first pair of toy-books was *John Gilpin*, whose horse shares the centre of the picture with his unfortunate rider (Fig. 4).

Although Caldecott obviously owed a great deal to Evans on the technical side, it is equally obvious

K. Hoddle

6

A. C. Cooper

Fig. 5 *Title-page of*
Marigold Garden by Kate
Greenaway, printed in colour by
Edmund Evans and published by
George Routledge and Sons,
London, 1885.
This collaboration between Kate
Greenaway and Evans surpassed
anything that had gone before.
She created a world in which
children felt entirely at home,
and he was able to translate
it into a commercial medium.
(Borough of Camden Libraries
and Arts Department.)

Fig. 6 *Title-page of Come*
Lasses and Lads, one of the
picture-book series illustrated by
Randolph Caldecott and
published by George Routledge
and Sons, London, 1883.
Artist's proof of the wood-
engraving. Caldecott made the
drawings for this series in black
and white, and was sent these
proofs, printed in brown, which
he filled in with up to five colours.
(Victoria and Albert Museum.)

that the artist had much to do with the choice of subjects. Of his sixteen titles in the series, five concerned horses and seven others were set in rural backgrounds. Evans may have suggested *The House That Jack Built* and *Hey Diddle Diddle* but it was surely Caldecott who chose *The Three Jovial Huntsmen* and *The Fox Jumps Over the Farmer's Gate.*

Caldecott was not quite forty when he died in February 1886. He had already intimated to Evans that the toy-books he had completed for the following Christmas season would be his last. With them, the whole series ended. Their popularity has never faded, and nearly one hundred years after their inception they are still in print; until very recently the original wood-blocks were still in use.

Caldecott also illustrated, for Evans to print, two of the best-known of Mrs. Ewing's stories for children, *Jackanapes* and *Daddy Darwin's Dovecote.* Both were published by the S.P.C.K. in 1884. Other illustrators of Mrs. Ewing's books include Gordon Browne (the son of Phiz who illustrated many of Dickens' novels) and George Cruikshank.

The combination in Caldecott of a great talent with a happy temperament gives his work the quality shared by all the best children's books – they appeal to young and old alike.

The father of Kate Greenaway (1846–1901) was a wood-engraver who frequently showed his daughter's drawings to Evans. Although it is possible that her first published work was the frontispiece to *Innocent Amusements* (1865), and despite her collaboration with Crane in a gaudy chromolithographic production in 1877, *The Quiver of Love,* she made no real mark until after a visit to Evans' family at Witley in Surrey.

She brought with her a collection of coloured drawings and verses which she had written to accompany them. Evans seized on these immediately. The outcome was *Under the Window,* issued in 1878 by Routledge in some trepidation at being committed by Evans to an edition of 20,000 copies. In the event, 70,000 were sold very

quickly and, with French and German editions, the 100,000 mark was probably reached (Fig. 1).

In 1885, with *Marigold Garden,* the collaborators surpassed anything that had gone before (Fig. 5). Between these two books came *Mother Goose* and *A Day in a Child's Life* (1881), *Little Ann* (1883) and *The Language of Flowers* (1884). In 1883 was published the first of the pretty *Almanacks,* which Kate Greenaway continued to produce annually until 1894–95.

Immortality is rather a strong term for her slender talent. She herself, with characteristic modesty, envied the superior quality and invention of Caldecott. She probably owed more to Evans than either Crane or Caldecott; in *Marigold Garden,* in particular, it is impossible to say how much of the design was due to Kate and how much was suggested by Evans. Nevertheless, she created a small world of her own in which children undoubtedly find themselves completely at home. Her '*A*' *Apple Pie* (1886) has been said to be 'the most popular book with children in libraries in America'.

Of the many other artists whose illustrated children's books deserve credit, space allows mention of only three others: Thomas Crane, Harrison Weir and Richard Doyle.

Thomas Crane, Walter's elder brother, was art director to the firm of Marcus Ward, and it was probably he who commissioned the books illustrated by Walter for that firm. He himself was capable of producing quite tolerable book decorations, usually in collaboration with his cousin, Ellen Houghton. Good examples of his work are *At Home* (1881), *Abroad* (1882) and *London Town* (1883), all published by Ward.

Harrison Weir, who had been an apprentice to George Baxter, specialised in animals and birds. He was one of the artists employed on the Routledge toy-books before Crane, producing, for example, *The Cats' Tea-Party,* with chromolithographs printed by Kronheim. He illustrated Mrs. Trimmer's *History of the Robins* (1869), for which his drawings were engraved on wood by Kate Greenaway's

7

Fig. 7 *I Saw Three Ships* by *Walter Crane. Pen, ink and water-colour drawing for a book-illustration.*
It is impossible to date Crane's series of toy-books accurately, but all were produced between 1864 and 1876.
(British Museum.)

father, and his own *Animal Stories* (1885) is charming.

Weir was born in 1826 and died in 1906. In 1850 he and John Absolon, a stage designer, supplied frontispieces for a *Treasury of Pleasure Books for the Young*, issued by that enterprising but luckless publisher, John Cundall. They were available plain or coloured by hand, and were reissued by Sampson Low in 1858, after Cundall's bankruptcy.

For the Christmas season of 1869 (the title-page is dated 1870), Evans produced William Allingham's poem *In Fairyland*, illustrated by Richard Doyle, a masterpiece of colour-printing, which was published by Longman's. Lucky were the children to whom it was given, for it cost a guinea and a half (about £10 in contemporary currency). It was, nevertheless, reprinted in 1875.

COLLECTORS' HINTS
All the books mentioned above as printed by Evans were originally published by Routledge. Any with the imprint of Warne or any other publisher are without value.

The Caldecott series are advertised on the back wrapper of each title. Obviously, no first edition advertises titles later than the previous one in the series.

The Crane toy-books are extremely scarce – the

Caldecotts much less so. The Crane 'Baby' books and the Greenaways are not at all easy to find in really fine condition. 🔣

MUSEUMS AND COLLECTIONS
Victorian children's books may be seen at the following:

CANADA
Toronto: Toronto Public Library
GREAT BRITAIN
London: Victoria and Albert Museum
U.S.A.
Cambridge, Mass: Houghton Library, Harvard University
Tallahassee, Fla: John Shaw Collection, Florida State University

FURTHER READING
The Reminiscences of Edmund Evans, edited and with a foreword by R. McLean, Oxford, 1967.
English Children's Books by Percy Muir, London, 1954.
An Artist's Reminiscences by Walter Crane, London, 1907.
Kate Greenaway by M. H. Spielman and G. S. Layard, London, 1905.
The Art of Walter Crane by P. G. Konody, London, 1902.
Randolph Caldecott by H. Blackburn, London, 1886.

1

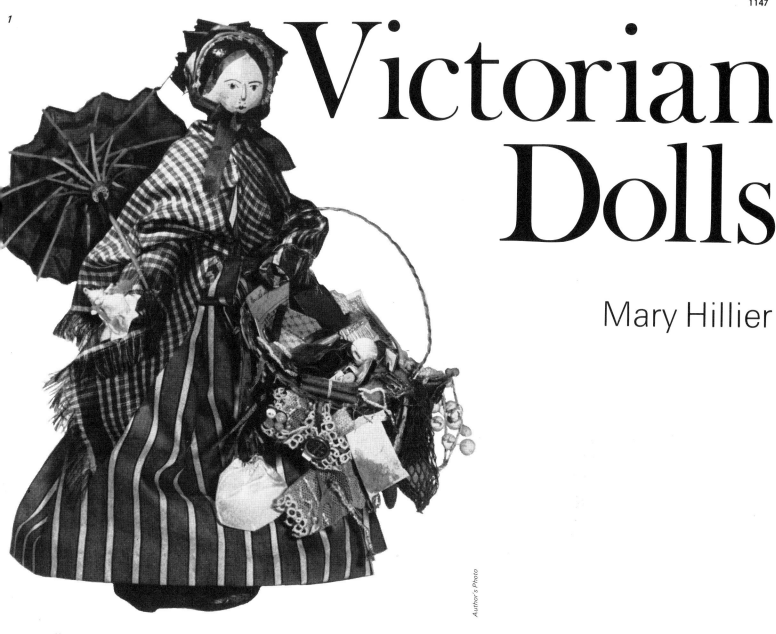

Victorian Dolls

Mary Hillier

Author's Photo

Fig. 1 **Pedlar-doll** *selling
miniature goods.
This type of woman pedlar with
a basket of goods and the
corresponding man with a tray
are among the most sought-after
of Victorian dolls. Among the
replicas of song-sheets, pins,
skeins of wool, ribbons and
baubles, there is often a
miniature jointed wooden doll.
(Stranger's Hall, Norwich.)*

**Witch-like fortune-tellers,
blue-eyed German dolls, families
of Parian miniature dolls and
milliners' models, all were played
with by Victorian children**

'The best of descriptions could not convey any idea
of the richly coloured silks and satins of the robes or
of the cunning needle art which has been expended
upon their embellishment, or of the delicate fancy
which has been employed with the happiest results.'

This eulogistic account concerns a family of dolls
dressed by Queen Victoria when she was a child
with the help of her Governess, Baroness Lehzen.
They represent real characters whom the little girl
had met in society, or stage characters from
performances in London theatres.

The dolls themselves are not remarkable, but they
are typical of the period and a good starting-
point for a survey of Victorian dolls. Such little
turned wooden dolls with pegged jointed limbs and
gaily painted features and hair were imported in
their thousands from Germany. From medieval
times, Nuremberg had been a great toy-making
city, acting as a commercial centre for the surrounding village districts such as Oberammergau,

Berchtesgaden and the Groden Valley, heavily
afforested areas where early ecclesiastical carving
skills had given place to toy production.

When Queen Victoria was a child, most European
play dolls were of carved or turned wood, varying
in size and quality according to price, but with the
Industrial Revolution new methods were introduced, and techniques which signalled the beginning of mass production began to be adopted. There
were better facilities for distribution and marketing
and above all there was a greater demand for toys
of all sorts.

Papier mâché, which had been used since medieval times for a variety of modelling purposes,
proved to be a very simply made, practical material
for dolls' heads, and improved techniques invented
in France and Germany which added thickening
and hardening ingredients produced an almost
unbreakable composition which could be shaped to
a great variety of forms.

Particularly popular were patterns reproducing
ladylike figures with coiffured heads or moulded
hats and bonnets (Fig. 9). The name of 'milliners'
models' has been attached to this class, possibly
often used to demonstrate the latest in fashion and
hair styles, but they were also popular playthings
for children and a useful opportunity for girls to
display their needlework skills.

The charity bazaar in Victorian times would often

Fig. 2 Left: *Mechanical doll rocking a baby by Roullet-Decamps of Paris, c.1900. Height 16 ins.*
Right: *Wax doll, German, 1871. Height 12 ins.*
Social reforms and the Great War of 1914–18 saw the end of this type of doll and the closing of many of the German and French doll-factories.
(Author's Collection.)

Fig. 3 *Two-faced bonnet doll in wicker cradle, German, 1880. Composition, height 12 ins. The two-faced doll had two moulded expressions, one laughing and one crying, which could be changed at will. (Author's Collection.)*

Fig. 4 *Wax doll, probably made by Charles Marsh, London, 1865. Height 28 ins. Unlike their German equivalents, which were made of papier mâché dipped in wax, these fine English dolls were cast in pure wax and never cracked from exposure to cold. (Mrs. Patrick Ogilvie Collection.)*

Fig. 5 *Paper doll and dresses produced by Hoods as an advertisement for their sarsaparilla, American, 1894. (Author's Collection.)*

feature such popular dressed dolls as old pedlar-women or witch-like fortune-tellers with crinolines of folded paper 'fortunes'. The pedlar, with wide-brimmed black hat, flowing red cloak and basket loaded with trinkets, must have been welcome in outlying villages, and in the load carried by the sought-after pedlar-doll there is often included the most miniature of jointed wooden dolls among the replicas of song-sheets, pins, skeins of wool, ribbons and baubles (Fig. 1).

It has never been satisfactorily explained just where or how the idea of providing dolls with porcelain heads evolved, but one must accept that the idea originated from the beautiful figurine and bust portraits of the German factories. Dolls' heads before the 1830s are rare and the earliest seem to have been produced at Meissen; examples exist with the famous crossed swords mark and others with the 'K.P.M.' of the State porcelain factory.

Crowned heads were modelled in porcelain

China is not an obvious material for fashioning toys, but it could be used in an especially decorative way and there is no doubt that the novelty was very popular. By the middle of the century the heavy clay pottery district of Thuringia, inheriting the earlier techniques, was producing a plentiful supply of sturdy china dolls in great variety. Typically, the German doll was black-haired, blue-eyed, rosy-cheeked with a sparkling glaze, but fair-haired types and many variations in hair styling were produced and there was a constant experimentation in novel patterns. China arms and legs as well as the head-and-shoulders china bust were stuck or sewn to a sewn leather body or even a jointed wooden torso to complete the dolls (Fig. 8). Many of the German potteries turned out a mixture of goods which included both household crocks and dolls' heads.

When Parian ware became popular for ornaments, the doll-makers followed suit and produced some of the most decorative dolls' heads ever made. Parian could produce a very clear-cut model, being unglazed, and was especially suitable for detail. Portrait-dolls became popular with an intriguing attention to decoration and even jewellery and details of costume. Queen Victoria herself was represented, as well as her beloved Prince Albert, the Empress Eugénie and Napoleon III, Franz Josef, Princess Alexandra and celebrated singers such as Jenny Lind.

Delightful families of Parian miniature dolls usurped the old-style wooden types, some of the latter doubtless being consigned to humbler roles below stairs. Fathers with black beards and whiskers, Mamas with piled up braided golden hair and ruched blouses set off by a purple necktie, all in tinted Parian, and families of ornamental children became popular.

The making and furnishing of dolls' houses was a Victorian recreation in which the whole family could be involved – girls dressing the inhabitants and boys setting to on fretwork furniture. Shops of the period provided an enormous range of tiny accessories and utensils as well as sheets of miniature patterned wallpaper and boxes of dolls. Even without accounts of the period it is clear from a glimpse into one of these enchanted microcosms how different was life in a Victorian household from the present day.

Solid and respectable, the rooms are shut off from the outside world by net and velvet curtains. Heavy mirrors and gold-framed pictures line the drawing-room, where Mama presides at the piano or work-table. Clocks and lamps and ornaments are all there in replica, even the tabby curled up in his basket. Down below in the huge kitchen with its heavy cooking-range and washing-copper, innumerable pots and pans and plate-lined dresser, Cook prepares some of those colourful simulated dainties stuck on cardboard dishes (which could be bought by the bagful).

The best of dolls' houses boasts a nursery with resident nurse, rocking-horse, cradle and numerous children. Dolls and toys were passed down in a large family, and many fine antiques owe their survival

to the fact that they were treated as 'best', or 'drawing-room' dolls which a child was allowed to handle only for short periods on special occasions under supervision.

In the first half of the nineteenth century the Germans were unquestionably the largest producers of various types of china dolls' heads. They had practically a monopoly, and the French dollmakers of the period used either papier-mâché or china heads from Germany to add to beautifully hand-stitched bodies of gusseted kid, and dressed them *à la Parisienne* to produce their *poupées modèles*, luxurious little fashion queens who often came complete with an additional trousseau in a fitted travelling-chest.

One of the first French potters to compete with the German market was Jacob Petit, who added a range of dolls' heads to his famous ornamental wares. Others followed, and there were many improvements in structure: swivel necks, sleeping eyes, moving arms and legs. There was a strong predilection among French makers to produce novelty mechanical dolls. As early as 1845 Nicholas Théroude produced a clockwork doll which moved its arms and looked from side to side as it rolled along on a three-wheeled platform; his firm patented many other clever mechanical dolls and automata.

Edison patented a china doll which sang nursery rhymes

One of the most famous of all walking dolls was the memorably named 'Autoperipatetikos', an American invention of 1862 with little feet which confidently propelled her along step by step. She was widely sold in England with a variety of different heads, her machinery encased in a bell-shaped crinoline. A rarer companion model was a zouave.

Another American success was the Goodwin walking doll of 1868 (Fig. 7), which wheeled a small pram, and a boy on a velocipede of 1870, giving publicity to the new-fangled tricycle. Many of the clever mechanical dolls of the period reflected the advance of science. In 1878, Edison patented a phonograph doll, anticipating the great role canned music would one day play in the entertainment of the young. The pretty china doll sang nursery rhymes by virtue of a little machine, the records for which could be changed, fitted inside her body.

Pretty dolls with heads of *bisque* were widely used for a range of ingenious automata worked by strong wind-up clockwork and usually performed to the strains of a musical-box hidden in the stand (Fig. 2). They form one of the most charming (and expensive) types of collectable dolls and include dancers, flower-sellers, musicians and magicians, as well as performing groups. The 1870s was in fact the golden age of dolls, and there was great competition in producing talking and walking dolls, even dolls that breathed, drank or whistled. Queen Victoria set a model of domesticity and family life that was copied in humbler homes, and even older girls played with dolls and imitated all the chores connected with them. Mrs. Leech in her *Childrens' Dressmaker* published special patterns for dolls' layettes. Manufacturers specialised in every sort of dolls' accessory, miniature furniture, tea-sets, and cooking stoves.

In a beauty contest of dolls, the French *bébés* (child-dolls rather than babies) reigned supreme. They had wigs of luxuriant silky hair to crown their rosy, *bisque* faces, and brilliant life-like glass eyes with lashes, well-defined eyebrows and strong jointed bodies and limbs. They came dressed in the latest Paris fashions with all the frills and furbelows of the period, pretty bonnets, tiny buckled shoes and kid gloves. These large and splendid dolls were in reality a sort of status symbol. Only the child of a wealthy parent could own such a precious and expensive toy.

Bru, Steiner and Jumeau were perhaps the foremost doll-making firms but it was a colossal industry and a whole district of Paris was occupied in the production of dolls. Much has been written about the famous dolls of Emile Jumeau made at

The best were expensive and in fact minor works of art involving careful craftsmanship (Fig. 4). The liquid wax was poured into two- or three-part moulds to form head and limbs and these were sewn to a stuffed fabric body by means of eyelet holes. Hair was set in the scalp in small tufts and the cheeks were polished and made to glow with added colour powder. Glass eyes were fixed behind cut-out sockets and the details of features were sculptured by hand. Nothing was more Victorian in sentiment, and the finished efforts often had a typically too-good-to-live look about them, an ethereal sweetness and pallor.

Possibly the method was originally introduced by immigrant model-makers. Two of the most famous wax doll-making families, the Montanaris and the Pierottis, were manufacturing dolls before 1850.

Fig. 6 **Fashion-plate** *showing little girls at play, from the* Journal des Demoiselles, *Paris, 1871. Hand-coloured engraving. (Author's Collection.)*

Montreuil on the outskirts of Paris. Inheriting a small doll-making business from his father, Jumeau built a modern factory in 1878 with up-to-date working conditions, and set out to produce dolls which enjoyed a higher reputation than any others. He won many medals at exhibitions all over the world; the great industrial fairs gave the doll-making firms vast publicity and obviously fanned the flames of competition – and piracy – between countries.

England was never a great doll-making country save in one respect, the wax doll. Whereas Germany produced a cheap type of wax doll which was no more than a papier-mâché moulded type dipped in wax to give it a complexion – a thin layer prone to crack from exposure to cold – there were numerous London makers who produced dolls with heads and limbs moulded from pure wax.

It would be unfair to depict just one side of the coin; if the fine stores displayed a variety of luxury dolls, the back streets, both in London and Paris, held wretched dwellings where the very poor earned a bare living making them. Mayhew drew attention to the plight of some of these poor toy-makers in a series of letters to the *Morning Chronicle* in 1850 and instanced in particular one family he found living in a bare candle-lit room. The man, whose appearance showed 'grinding poverty', moulded papier-mâché dolls with the help of his young children and his wife who also sewed leather bodies. He looked upon two shillings and sixpence as a good day's work and, with the coffin of one small child still in the room awaiting burial, said piteously: 'The children of the people who will be happy with my dolls, little think under what circumstances they are made'.

Fig. 7 *Goodwin walking doll, 1868. Height 11 ins. After 1845, when Nicholas Théroude first produced a clockwork doll, many different mechanical dolls were patented.* (London Museum.)

Fig. 9 *Milliner's Model with elaborate coiffure, German, 1827. Papier mâché, height 23½ ins. Intended to demonstrate the latest fashions and hair-styles, these model dolls were also popular playthings for children.* (London Museum.)

Fig. 8 *China doll said to represent Princess Alexandra, German, 1863. Details in colour and lustre, height 16½ ins. The bodies of china dolls were made of leather or jointed wood.* (London Museum.)

MUSEUMS AND COLLECTIONS

Victorian dolls may be seen at the following:

FRANCE
Paris: Musée des Arts Décoratifs

GREAT BRITAIN
Edinburgh: Museum of Childhood
Keighley: Cliffe Castle Museum
London: Bethnal Green Museum
 London Museum
Norwich: Stranger's Hall
Rottingdean: Toy Museum
Worthing: Museum and Art Gallery
York: Castle Museum

WEST GERMANY
Nuremberg: Toy Museum

U.S.A.
New York: New York Historical Society
 Museum

FURTHER READING

Dolls and Dollmakers by Mary Hillier, London, 1968.
The Collector's Encyclopedia of Dolls by D. S., E. A. and E. J. Coleman, New York, 1968.
Dolls by John Noble, London, 1967.
English Dolls, Effigies and Puppets by Alice K. Early, London, 1955.
English Dolls' Houses of the Eighteenth and Nineteenth Centuries by Vivien Greene, London, 1955.

K. Hoddle

Toys of the Victorian Era

Mary Speaight

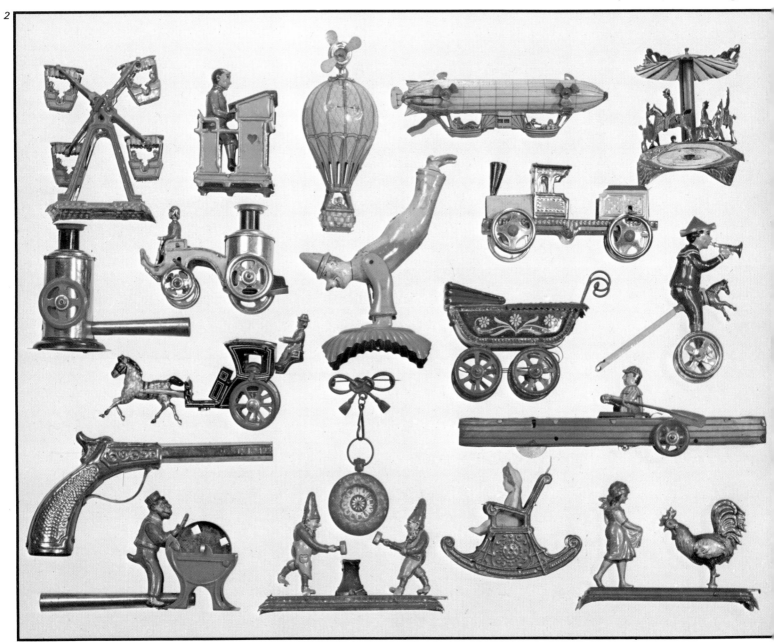

2

K. Hoddle

Fig. 1 **Toy theatre** by Benjamin
Pollock from a design of about
1850. Wood with hand-coloured
and varnished paper stage-front
and orchestra.
The stage is set with Scene Five,
the Palace of King Block, from
Sleeping Beauty in the Wood.
On stage are the King's
bodyguard, the King and Queen,
Hocus Pocus and Baron Sprout.
(Pollock's Toy Museum,
London.)

Fig. 2 **Penny toys** made in
Germany for the English market,
c.1890. Painted tin, maximum
height $3\frac{1}{2}$ ins.
Many of the cheap toys sold by
street-traders in England were
imported from Germany. The
pedlars would stand in the
gutters of the streets around
St. Paul's in London, their trays
full of small toys of all kinds.
(London Museum.)

Fig. 3 **Rocking-horse**, English,
early nineteenth century. Carved
and painted wood, height 4 ft.
This horse originally had a leather
saddle and bridle.
(Bethnal Green Museum,
London.)

From simple German penny toys to
optical devices of great complexity
and cost such as the
Phenakistiscope and the
Zoetrope, the Victorian child
enjoyed a wide and attractive
range of playthings

The Victorian era was a golden age for toys. From
the beginning of the nineteenth century there was a
rapid development in the number and variety of
toys available. Increasing technical knowledge,
hand in hand with a diversity of skills, was helpful
in creating many new amusements for the young;
while the expansion of the middle class meant that
more and more parents were able to buy these playthings for their children.

The rich bought their toys in the bazaars and
fashionable arcades; the poor bought theirs at fairs
and street-markets. One of the most popular
expeditions for Victorian children was a visit to the
famous Lowther Arcade, on the north side of the
Strand, which was lined with shops selling fancy
ornaments and toys of every kind. A painting of
about 1860 shows this Aladdin's Cave thronged
with benevolent parents, aunts and uncles escorting
eager-eyed children. All the traditional toys are
there: dolls and dolls' houses, trumpets and drums,
buckets and spades, hoops and tops, kites with
faces, the Noah's Ark, a rocking-horse with leather
harness and smaller horses with striped wooden
barrel-bodies resting on spindly legs, maned and
tailed with strips of furry hide, waiting to be
pushed or pulled away.

Cheap toys were sold by street-traders from
barrows and stalls. Many of the toys they sold
were imported from Germany, and others were
made in the back streets of English towns. Henry
Mayhew tells of some of the toy-makers he inter-

viewed in London, in letters published in the
Morning Chronicle during December 1850: 'The
Bristol toys [made of wood] are the common toys
made for the children of the poor, and generally
retail at a penny. They were first made in Bristol,
but have been manufactured in London for the last
fifty years. Bristol toys are carts, horses, omnibuses,
chaises, steamers and suchlike – nearly all wheel-
toys . . . the toy is cut with a knife, and fixed
together with glue, then painted. All my toys go to
the poor, and are a sort of luxury to the children'.

A particular place where street-traders con-
gregated to sell these cheap toys was in the area of
London around St. Paul's, and it was to Ludgate
Hill that parents and children in the '80s and '90s
made their annual pilgrimage to buy small toys to
hang on the Christmas tree.

Charles Dickens describes some of the cheap
toys on 'that pretty German toy, a Christmas Tree
. . . There were rosy-cheeked dolls, hiding behind
the green leaves, and there were real watches (with
movable hands, at least, and an endless capacity of
being wound up) dangling from innumerable twigs;
there were tables, chairs, bedsteads, wardrobes
and various other articles of domestic furniture,
perched among the boughs, as if in preparation for
some fairy housekeeping'; he notices, too, 'the sets
of platters each with its own peculiar delicacy, as a
ham or turkey, glued tightly on to it', and 'the
tumbler with his hands in his pockets, who
wouldn't lie down'.

Dickens goes on to recall another favourite
Victorian toy – was it because it met the requirements of Sunday as well as weekdays that it was so
popular? 'O, the wonderful Noah's Ark! It was not
found seaworthy when put in a washing-tub, and
the animals were crammed in at the roof, and
needed to have their legs well shaken down before
they could be got in, even there – and then, ten to
one but they began to tumble out at the door, which
was but imperfectly fastened with a wire latch – but
what was *that* against it!'

A group of toy-makers who were very active in

Fig. 4 *Le Jeu du Ménage* from *Les Jouets*, 1895. *Engraving. In France as in England, playing house was a favourite occupation of little girls. Elaborate furniture was available for this pastime, such as the complete kitchen, dining-room set and tea-service lavished on this lucky doll.*

Fig. 5 *Zoetrope*, *English, second half of the nineteenth century. Metal drum revolving on a metal spindle in a wooden stand. A popular toy of the later Victorian era, the Zoetrope could be fitted with various paper strips such as the man on a donkey in this example (see also Fig. 6). A number of children at the same time could peer through the slits when the drum was revolved, and have the illusion of a moving image.* (Pollock's Toy Museum.)

Fig. 6 *Strips for a Zoetrope. Printed paper. See Figure 5.* (Pollock's Toy Museum.)

Fig. 7 Left: *Group of soldiers*, *Britain's, English, 1893–99. Hollow-cast and painted alloy of tin and lead. These are early Britain's models of a wounded soldier with nurses and a medical officer, three Guards bandsmen and a Rifle Brigade soldier. They are much smaller than those produced after the Boer War.*
Right: *Group of soldiers by Heyde, Dresden, late nineteenth century. Solid-cast and painted lead. Until they were ousted by the great popularity of Britain's soldiers, German examples were common in England. These models show nurses tending wounded soldiers. They are cast with German uniforms, but painted with British military colours for the export market.* (Tradition, London, S.W.1.)

Fig. 8 *Noah's Ark with one hundred figures, English, c.1860. Carved and painted wood, height of ark 10 ins. These sets were particularly popular since they were appropriate for Sunday as well as weekday play.* (London Museum.)

4

5

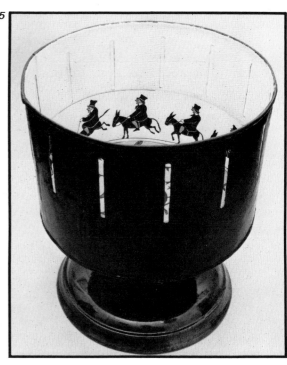

Mary Evans Picture Library

the early years of the century were the print-sellers. They produced cards, table-games, jigsaw puzzles and toy theatres.

Jigsaws, known as 'dissected puzzles', were first introduced towards the end of the eighteenth century. The main publishers at the beginning of the following century were Edward Wallis and William Darton, producing chiefly maps and pictorial histories. Darton issued as well a series of moral poems with the titles *My Mother*, *My Grandmother*, *My Bible*, each illustrated by six hand-coloured engravings. Wallis, in about 1830, published the *Liverpool and Manchester Railway*. In 1840, A. Park, a toy-theatre publisher, brought out a dramatic puzzle, *Edward Oxford firing at Her Majesty*, depicting the attempted assassination of Queen Victoria.

These were followed by William Spooner and John Betts. Spooner, a publisher of high-class workmanship who used hand-coloured lithographs, made a speciality of the production of everyday commodities with titles such as *The Sugar Plantation* and *A Loaf of Bread*. John Betts, a prolific publisher, produced mostly maps and Bible stories, and included a key picture and booklet with his puzzles. There were besides many unknown publishers making puzzles, often of poor workmanship and covering a multitude of lively subjects such as the Lord Mayor's show, the coronation and wedding of Queen Victoria, the seaside, souvenirs of the Great Exhibition and pictures from children's story-books.

Pictures for dissected puzzles were first mounted on mahogany, but soon whitewood, which was cheaper, began to be used instead. The puzzles were cut with only the edges interlocking and sold in well-constructed boxes with sliding lids; again, these were made at first in mahogany, with small neatly printed labels, but well before 1850 white-wood was used for the boxes which were made shiny with varnish and bore large, brightly coloured labels.

'Out of this delight springs the toy theatre', wrote Charles Dickens, recalling the magic of pantomime. 'There it is with its familiar proscenium, and ladies in feathers, in the boxes! – and all its

attendant occupation with paste and glue, and gum, and water colours, in the getting up of *The Miller and His Men*'. The toy theatre was an absorbing interest for boys of middle-class families, especially where there was an enthusiasm for acting and the stage. The characters and scenery were reproduced from current productions and sold in the stationers' shops for a penny plain and twopence coloured. The first sheets were published in 1811 and the first toy theatre was made in 1813 by William West. Henry Mayhew reports West's own words: 'I am a maker of children's theatres ... I was the first in the line ... My parents used to be at Covent Garden theatre and I took it in my head to have a print done of *Mother Goose* ... At first, you see, we didn't do any but the principal characters in a piece, ... After that we was asked by the customers for theayters to put the characters in, so I got up the print of a stage front'.

The theatres had little tin footlights to contain wicks burning colza-oil. The characters were stuck on card, cut out and pushed on and off the stage on wire slides. The plays were adapted from real plays performed in the London theatres. West said: '*The Miller and His Men* has sold better than any other play I ever published ... It's the last scene, with the grand explosion of the mill, as pleases the young 'uns, uncommon. The next most taking play out of my shop has been *Blue Beard*. That the boys like for the purcession over the mountains – a-coming to take Fatima away.'

There were about a hundred publishers who issued between them three hundred different plays. After West came Green and Skelt, then Redington and Pollock. The toy theatre had its heyday in the 1830s and '40s, with children of middle-class families playing with them in their nurseries and parlours. From 1875, Benjamin Pollock was selling toy theatres in his shop in Hoxton Street, in one of the poorer quarters of London, and at the end of Queen Victoria's reign children in the back rooms of humbler homes were still performing plays such as *Aladdin*, *The Sleeping Beauty*, *Blackbeard the Pirate* and *The Miller and His Men*, which remained the most popular of them all.

The name of Britain is associated with toy

soldiers in every Englishman's mind, but many toy soldiers were made before his time. In the early years of the nineteenth century, painted wooden soldiers were well known and enjoyed by, among others, the Brontë family. Then there were card-board soldiers, made from cheap colouring sheets put out by print-sellers; mounted on small blocks of wood, they could be stood in ranks to make an imposing army. Throughout the nineteenth century there were many German firms making flat and solid lead soldiers. Two well-known firms were Haffner and Heyde; both made well-designed and well-painted soldiers in a wide range of types and postures, and they were imported into England in large numbers.

But these lead soldiers were inevitably heavy. Britain, who introduced hollow-cast soldiers in 1893, had first set up in business in 1850, putting clockwork propelled animals on the market. It was in order to expand his business that he marketed a new invention – the first hollow-cast toy soldier. It was made of an alloy; it was light, quick in production and accurately painted. Although initially these models were viewed with suspicion, they eventually swept the market and completely replaced the German solid soldiers. Britain's first line was the Life Guards, soon to be followed by the Grenadier Guards and a kilted Highland regiment – lines which have remained popular to this day.

Toys reflect the age in which they are made, and any new discovery or invention produces a new toy. The steam age was reflected in this way and a toy train was an exciting present for a small boy in the 1830s. An early model is the little painted wooden train in the London Museum, and another is a tin train with the name 'Stephenson' marked on the engine. Then came the clockwork models and even real miniature steam-engines.

The mass production of clockwork toys began in about 1850. Besides trains, clockwork was used to make a tricyclist ride around in erratic circles, a bear to walk and turn its head from side to side, and a pair of negro dolls to jig about on a box. A moving toy listed in the catalogue of the Great Exhibition was: 'A mechanical toy of an English farm with figures, a threshing machine, windmill, etc., in action'. Mayhew reports an interview with a fancy toymaker: 'Fancy toys are mechanical and moving toys . . . My toys . . . include animals of all descriptions – donkeys, horses, cows, cats, elephants, lions, tigers (I could make giraffes but they're not in demand), dogs and pigs'. His room, Mayhew says, 'presented an accumulation of materials – paper, paste, wires, gilding, wood, pasteboard, leather, and other things, mixed up with instruments for nice admeasurement. The fancy toymaker's appearance was that of a hearty jovial man'. He really indicates the excitement of his job when he says: 'If I think of inventing a new toy I often can't sleep from thinking of it'.

The Victorian family, gathered together in the long winter evenings, often enjoyed some kind of pictorial plaything. The magic lantern had been known for several centuries, but now simple devices were used to give the pictures movement. Hand-painted glass slides were set in wooden frames and, by sliding one piece of glass behind another, a staring tiger slowly rolled his eyes from side to side; by pushing a lever up and down a clown skipped; by winding a handle a volcano erupted. Toy lanterns with small slides using the

Mary Evans Picture Library

10

K. Hoddle

a movement. The disc was spun on a spindle in front of a mirror while the viewer looked through the slits and saw the figure spring into movement. Thus a frog hopped over the grass or the face of a monster approached and receded.

The disadvantage of the Phenakistiscope was that only one person could view at a time; before long came a further development with the Zoetrope. The Zoetrope, a metal drum pierced with a number of slits, was revolved on a metal spindle in a wooden stand. A paper strip the length of the circumference and half the depth of the drum, again bearing a figure in various stages of a movement, was placed inside around the edge. As the drum was rotated, a number of viewers saw the figure in action; a horse jumped fences or a boy turned somersaults. Further scientific experiments produced more realistic and complicated moving picture toys, leading eventually to the invention of the cinema (Fig. 5).

Then, as now, children enjoy toys that released their energy, like games of skipping and hoop-bowling; games that developed skills, like top-whipping and kite-flying; that presented a challenge, like putting together a jigsaw puzzle and sailing a boat; or that fired the imagination, like toy soldiers and the toy theatre.

MUSEUMS AND COLLECTIONS

Victorian toys may be seen at the following:
GREAT BRITAIN
Edinburgh: Museum of Childhood
Leeds: City Museum
London: Bethnal Green Museum
London Museum
Pollock's Toy Museum
Rottingdean: Toy Museum

FURTHER READING

The World of Toys by Robert Culff, London, 1969.
Juvenile Drama: The History of the English Toy Theatre by George Speaight, London, 1969.
Two Hundred Years of Jigsaw Puzzles, catalogue with introduction by Linda Hannas, London, 1968.
A History of Toys by Antonia Fraser, London, 1966.
Movement in Two Dimensions by Olive Cook, London, 1963.
Model Soldiers by John Garratt, London, 1959.

Fig. 9 **Play horses** *from an advertisement in* The Ironmonger Diary and Text Book, *1889, for Dunkley's rocking-horses, prams and tricycles.*

Fig. 10 **Clockwork bear,** *English, second half of the nineteenth century. Covered with brown fur. This delightful beast walks, stops, opens its mouth and growls.*
(Bethnal Green Museum.)

same methods enabled children to give their own magic lantern shows.

During the nineteenth century, experiments based on the phenomenon of the persistence of vision produced a steady development in the moving-picture toy. In 1825 a new invention appeared in the shops, a box labelled 'Thaumatropical Amusement'. The Thaumatrope was a small paper disc with different objects drawn on each side of it and thin cords attached at each side. When the cords, held one in each hand between finger and thumb, were twirled, a bird from one side appeared in the cage on the other. In 1832 the Phenakistiscope appeared on the market. This was a large cardboard disc with deep notches cut around the edge. Between each of the ten, or sometimes twenty, notches were figures in different stages of

William Gaunt

THE AESTHETIC MOVEMENT

AFFILIATING AN ÆSTHETE.

Pilcox, a promising young Pharmaceutical Chemist, has modelled from memory an Heroic Group, in which Mrs. Cimabue Brown is represented as the Muse of this Century, crowning Postlethwaite and Maudle as the Twin Gods of its Poetry and Art.

Postlethwaite. "No loftiah Theme has evah employed the Sculptah's chisel!"

Maudle. "Distinctly so. Only work on in *this* reverent spirit, Mr. Pilcox, and you will achieve the *Truly Great!*"

Mrs. Cimabue Brown. "Nay, you *have* achieved it! Oh, my young Friend, do you not know that you are a Heaven-born Genius?" *Poor Pilcox.* "I do!" [*Gives up his pestle and mortar, and becomes a hopeless Nincompoop for life.*

2

Museum Photo

Ridiculed by press and public alike, the Aesthetic Movement in England sought to bring beauty to an industrial age and quality to a period of mass production

In the course of the nineteenth century's vast industrial and commercial growth, beauty had been lost. This was the verdict of contemporary critics and the thought behind what is known as the Aesthetic Movement, a reaction in England in the second half of the century against the ideas and tastes of a prosperous middle class, insensitive or imperfectly educated in matters of art. It was an effort also to counter the ugliness that seemed to have almost automatically developed in the products of the factory.

In one aspect, the Movement was the endeavour of artists and craftsmen to rediscover a beauty through the standards they applied to their own work. Another aspect was the kind of connoisseurship which is implied in the term 'aestheticism' – a tendency away from active production. The social order which Thomas Carlyle and Matthew Arnold branded as 'Philistine' on the general ground of its being smugly impervious to 'culture', and which in matters of art was subject to the thunderous exhortations of John Ruskin, was not uniformly unresponsive.

A section of society, at least, showed a

3

4

Fig. 1 (Frontispiece) *Affiliating an Aesthete by George du Maurier (1834–96) in* Punch, *June 19, 1880.*
Du Maurier gleefully satirised such Aesthetic figures as Swinburne, Rossetti and Oscar Wilde in his cartoons for Punch *throughout this period.*

Fig. 2 *The Golden Stairs by Edward Burne-Jones (1833–98), 1880. Oil on canvas.*
In this influential picture, the troop of ethereally refined maidens are as little Victorian in dress and general appearance as could be imagined. It was exhibited in 1880 at the Grosvenor Gallery, centre for the Aesthetic in painting.
(Tate Gallery, London.)

Fig. 3 *Dish by William de Morgan (1839–1917), late nineteenth century. Earthenware painted with a peacock pattern in 'Persian' colours.*
The peacock was a frequent motif of De Morgan's Persian style; he was no doubt inspired by the Anatolian pots at the South Kensington Museum.
(Victoria and Albert Museum, London.)

Fig. 4 *The Orchard, Chorley Wood, Hertfordshire, designed by Charles Voysey (1857–1941), 1899.*
A designer of informal, intimate country houses, Voysey had a great influence on domestic and rural architecture up to World War I. Like many designers of the Aesthetic Movement, he created all the furniture and details such as the metalwork and fireplaces for his houses as well as the basic design.

Fig. 5 *Oscar Wilde by Carlo Pellegrini (1839–89) for* Vanity Fair, *c.1885.*
Working as a caricaturist for Vanity Fair *under the pseudonym of 'Ape' for many years, Carlo Pellegrini created deathless images of many of the renowned characters of the day, of whom Wilde was perhaps the most notorious. Self-styled 'professor of aesthetics', Wilde was perhaps the greatest populariser, often in a negative sense, of the principles of the Aesthetic Movement.*

willingness to reform its taste in works of art and the decorative accessories of the home on the lines prescribed by Aesthetic mentors. A fashion was started, but was not immune from Philistine retaliation in the ridicule that grew uproarious in the 1880s.

Much earlier, the Pre-Raphaelites and their following had taken a heroic initiative as critics of prevailing Victorian standards and advocates of idealistic alternatives. The Pre-Raphaelite Brotherhood was, even in the middle of the century, taking its stand against the trivial pictorial anecdotes and humours that entertained the *bourgeois*. In the mystic combination of portraiture and allegory. Rossetti bequeathed his ideal female figure to an aesthetic succession.

Ethereally refined, and in dress and general appearance as little Victorian as could be imagined, was the troop of maidens in Edward Burne-Jones' *The Golden Stairs*, exhibited in 1880 at the Grosvenor Gallery, centre of the Aesthetic in painting. But painting was not solely in question. The second phase of Pre-Raphaelitism, in which William Morris came to the fore, widened the sphere of operations to combat what was deemed ugly in every form.

This was the task of Morris's firm of 'fine art workmen', launched in the 1860s and particularly successful in the following four decades. Instead of massive and pretentious furniture, Morris turned to simple types adapted from traditional, rural models, such as the Sussex ladder-back chair. His delightful wallpapers and chintzes showed that

5

Mansell Collection

pattern need not be a dull copy of Renaissance motifs and that clear colours were an improvement on dusky reds and browns. He helped to establish a style of lightweight, ebonised furniture and of floral ornament applicable to various surfaces and, by his affirmation that art should be as much a factor in useful handicrafts as in easel paintings, set an example which inspired many others.

The career of the brilliant designer of ceramics, William de Morgan, provides an example. Contact with Morris helped to convert him from the discouraged student of painting at the Royal Academy Schools to the enthusiastic potter whose tiles and lustre dishes came to be coveted by the advanced in appreciation. He was one of the new race of artist-craftsmen, although he was not involved in the organised activities of the Art Workers' Guild, founded in 1884, or the closely related Arts and Crafts Exhibition Society that followed in 1888. Walter Crane, the first President of the Art Workers' Guild, was a key figure of the period. His clear-cut style and areas of flat colour proved appropriate to a range of decorative purposes extending from designs for wallpaper to the illustration of children's books in which, along with Kate Greenaway, he may be said to have begun a new era.

The Aesthetic Movement was fed from a variety of sources. Charles L. Eastlake's *Hints on Household Taste*, published in 1868, was influential though the specimens of domestic furniture illustrated were prim and curious reminders of the Gothic Revival. The South Kensington Museum lured the eclectic with the amazing wealth of designs remaining from the Great Exhibition – no doubt its Anatolian pots inspired William de Morgan's Persian style. The Japanese taste was an exotic infiltration, a vogue created by the interest of collectors in Far Eastern art, by the impressive Japanese section of the Exhibition of 1862, and by the miscellany of imports at Farmer and Rogers' Oriental Warehouse in London.

Whistler's Nocturnes provoked Ruskin's petulant libel

Variety was in consequence a mark of the Aesthetic interior. It is possible to imagine the combination of an Eastlake sideboard, bearing a sumptuous dish with a sunflower or peacock pattern by De Morgan; Morris wallpaper and chairs; Japanese fans over the mantelpiece and objects of bamboo in odd corners. One may imagine the lady of the house in Aesthetic garb – the loose, flowing gown that opposed conventional Victorian fashion, in the style approved by painters of both Pre-Raphaelite and classical leanings – looking soulfully towards the wall-brackets of the kind designed by Thomas Jeckyll and holding a treasured piece of oriental porcelain.

An indifference to this social Aestheticism and a different view of art's place in the scheme of things were qualities of the redoubtable James McNeill Whistler. He derived his conception of beauty from such European masters as Degas, who assigned no moral or social purpose to art, and from Far Eastern artists who, whatever their subject or medium, were superbly intelligible in form and colour alone. A fastidious selection and a scrupulous regard for purely visual harmonies and effects characterised the Nocturnes and portraits of the 1870s, so

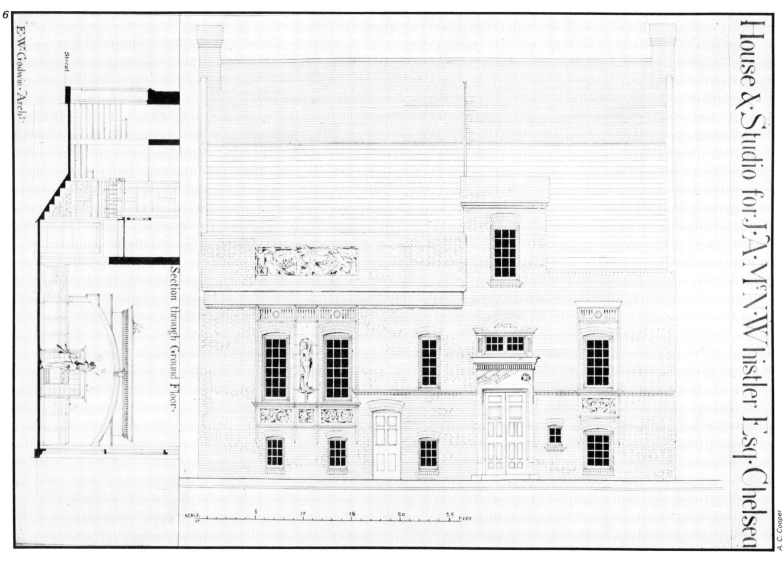

E·W·Godwin·Arch:

Street

Section through Ground Floor.

SCALE | 5 | 10 | 15 | 20 | 25 | FEET

A. C. Cooper

Fig. 6 **Plan** *for the front elevation of The White House and studios in Tite Street, Chelsea, designed for James McNeill Whistler by E. W. Godwin (1833–1886), 1877–78. Pen and ink. Whistler's house was as simple in external style as the Chelsea authorities allowed, and inside as light as the average Victorian interior was dark. (Victoria and Albert Museum.)*

Fig. 7 *La Dame aux Camélias by Aubrey Beardsley (1872–98), from* The Yellow Book, *Vol. III, 1894. Drawing, later tinted in colour. There was a strong element of decadence in much of Beardsley's work, often French in inspiration and in a special sense related to Aestheticism. (Tate Gallery.)*

Fig. 8 **The Peacock Garden,** *wallpaper by Walter Crane (1845–1915), 1889. Colour printed. (Victoria and Albert Museum.)*

distinct from the Victorian liking for elaboration as to provoke Ruskin's petulant attack which led to the famous action for libel in 1878.

Whistler would certainly have rejected the description of 'Aesthete', which indeed he used as a term of contempt, but he had strict aesthetic rules of order, spacing and carefully considered tonality which were manifested not only in his pictures but in the house in Tite Street, which he designed in conjunction with the architect E. W. Godwin (described by Max Beerbohm as the 'first of the aesthetes'). The White House was as simple in external style as the Chelsea authorities allowed and inside as light as the average Victorian interior was dark. His *penchant* for yellow was such that Charles Augustus Howell said that being inside Whistler's house was like being inside an egg.

The defects of English arts and crafts stood out for Whistler with awful clarity. He was ferociously sarcastic about the typical Academy subject picture and no less so about the idealistic craftsman whom he insisted on regarding as an inferior being. 'Can you forgive a plate for a peculiar shine?', was his remark on De Morgan lustre.

From a different standpoint, the Aesthetic Movement became the object of Philistine derision, especially when, at the end of the 1870s, Oscar Wilde made his startling London debut as 'professor of aesthetics'. His was a remarkably composite attitude, made up of the earnestness of Ruskin and Morris, sharpened by a seasoning of Whistlerian wit; the devout contemplation of the beautiful, recommended by Walter Pater, the literary proto-

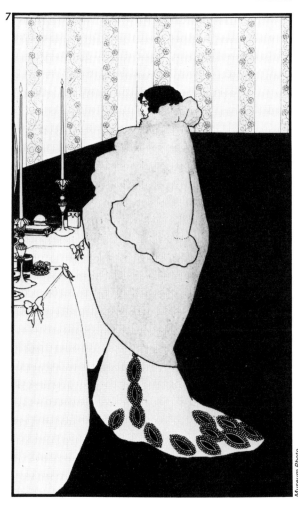

Museum Photo

8

A. C. Cooper

Fig. 9 *The High Art Maiden,* songbook cover for a
satirical song about the Aesthetic Movement by
Herbert Harraden, late nineteenth century.
Prominence is given-here to the sunflower and the lily,
two ubiquitous hallmarks of the Aesthetic Movement.

9

Mary Evans Picture Library

type of the university aesthete; the Pre-Raphaelite
nature-worship as represented by the symbolic lily
'held in a medieval hand'. Even his velvet jacket
and velveteen knickerbockers reflected the aversion
of painters to Victorian dress.

In the 1880s George du Maurier gleefully substi-
tuted Wilde as a target for his jibes in *Punch* against
the affectations of culture, instead of figures in
the 1870s satirising Rossetti and Swinburne. This
farcical picture of the Aesthetic Movement was
completed in 1881 by the Gilbert and Sullivan
comic opera *Patience*, in which Wilde clearly
figures as the absurdly posturing Bunthorne.
Although still undeniably amusing, the opera has
tended to perpetuate the idea of the Aesthetic
Movement as no more than a series of poses, and to
obscure its serious creative side.

The eclecticism of the movement had its late
example in the drawings of Aubrey Beardsley.
He began like any Pre-Raphaelite with his illustrations for *Morte d'Arthur* in the manner of Burne-
Jones. But the sight of Whistler's Peacock Room
turned him towards the *Japonaiserie* of his illustrations to Wilde's *Salome*. From his reading of French
literature his work assumed an element of *déca-
dence* in the sense related to Aestheticism, implying
that pursuit of strange and exquisite sensations
described by J. K. Huysmans in his novel *A Rebours*.
Beardsley heralded the extravagance of Art
Nouveau, although the so-called 'new art' of the
1890s and 1900s had an earnest arts and crafts
aspect in which the continuation of the Aesthetic
Movement may be discerned.

ARTHUR NEGUS COLLECTORS' ITEM

WILLIAM BRITAIN'S TOY SOLDIERS

The last decade of Queen Victoria's reign was the most splendid in the history of the Empire. Salisbury was Prime Minister, Curzon was Viceroy of India and novelists like G. A. Henty urged British boys 'to be bold, straightforward and ready to play a man's part – not to be milksops'. The passion for the Empire was so great that in 1893 the London firm of William Britain decided to launch a series of model soldiers illustrating the different regiments of the British and Dominions forces.

The success of this range was immediate; Lord Roberts bought a complete set, H. G. Wells wrote a book, *Little Wars,* about model warfare, and no British lad was content without his box of Britain's soldiers. In the years before the Great War, Britain's enlarged their range to include the leading continental armies, and in the inter-war period they were so well abreast of their field that they were the first company outside Germany to produce models of the new German Reichswehr. Britain's ceased the production of new figures after the coronation in 1953.	Their hollow case lead figures of imperial heroes gave way to plastic models of U.S. Combat Groups.

Collecting Hints

The earlier models and castings are the most valuable; the oldest figures are mounted on a circular rather than a rectangular base. Look for the stamp in the bottom of the base: 'Copyright Wm. Britain' puts the figure before 1912, and the simple legend 'Britains Ltd.' puts it before 1937. Thereafter, 'Made in England' was added. The rarest sets of all are the Indian Army elephant gun, the General Service Wagon and figures from the Boer War.

Prices

Some groups fetch as much as £20; individual figures range between 50p for a battered footman and £5 for an immaculate hussar.

Above: ***German soldiers in a personnel carrier,*** *Elastolin factory, 1937, £35.*
Below: ***Box of soldiers of the 1890s,*** *Britain, £3.*
Bottom: ***Army ambulance,*** *1912, £15.*
Front: ***South Australian lancer,*** *£2.50.*

Two typical ***'pigeon chest' infantry men,*** *£2.* ***'Gun to shoot' soldier*** *which may be fired by placing ammunition on the spring, pulling back and releasing, £5.*
Back: ***Boer infantry soldier,*** *£2.50.* ***Arab camel corps,*** *£1.25. All by Britain.*

Opposite: ***Napoleonic kettle drummer*** *by Lucotte in imitation of Britain's style. £10.*

John Houston

Art Workers in Metal

4

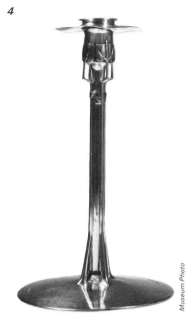

Fig. 1 **Decanter,** *designed by William Burges and made by Richard A. Green for James Nicholson, London, 1865–66. Glass bottle mounted in chased and parcel-gilt silver, set with amethysts, opals, malachite and other semi-precious stones as well as with ancient Greek and Roman coins, inscribed around the neck 'JAMES NICHOLSON ANNO DOMINI MDCCCLXV' (Victoria and Albert Museum, London.)*

Fig. 2 **Christening cup,** *designed by Richard Redgrave R.A., made by S. H. and D. Glass, 1849, reissued by Harry Emanuel, London, 1865. Silver. Designed for the Summerly's Art Manufactures in 1848, this fine cup was later shown at the Great Exhibition of 1851. (Victoria and Albert Museum.)*

Fig. 3 **Bowl,** *designed by C. R. Ashbee (1863–1942) and made by the Guild of Handicraft Ltd., 1895–96. Silver, embossed and chased with a leaf design, with cast legs. (Victoria and Albert Museum.)*

Fig. 4 **Candlestick,** *one of a pair designed by R. C. Silver and made by W. H. Haseler, Birmingham, for Liberty & Co., 1906–7. Hand-raised silver. The design for these superb candlesticks was first published in Studio, Vol. XIX, 1900. (Victoria and Albert Museum.)*

In the late nineteenth century both hand-wrought and machine-made metalwork of quality and originality was produced in Britain by designers and craftsmen of considerable merit

As architect and author, Catholic convert, designer of furniture, jewellery and metalwork, Augustus Welby Northmore Pugin (1812–52) raised the gothic style from an optional extra to an article of faith. In so doing, his problem was not merely to gain acceptance for a style, but to find craftsmen skilled enough to carve wood and stone and to fashion metal in a truly gothic manner. It was important that there should be a revival, not only of a medieval style, but also of the necessary skills. England's advanced industrial revolution had already cheapened manufacture, craftsmanship had all but disappeared and designers had not yet learnt to create forms suitable for mechanical production.

Rolling-mills, Sheffield plate, die-stamping, fly-punching and electro-plating had, by 1850, created a large amount of low-priced silver and silver plate. Mechanically complicated forms imitated misunderstood prototypes, Grecian or gothic, rococo or Elizabethan. Sometimes a single object would be touched by several historical styles, an amalgam which Pugin called 'the Sheffield eternal'.

The Schools of Design, Henry Cole's *Journal of Design and Manufacture* and the lessons of the Great Exhibition had helped to create an atmosphere of design reform. In 1852 *Metal Work and its Artistic Design* by Matthew Digby Wyatt (1820–77) was published; the author echoed the dull good sense of the circle round Henry Cole, but his designs for silver were, paradoxically, affected to a considerable extent by the vulgar fashions and debased styles which he criticised.

Digby Wyatt, for all his liberal views on improved design, still moved in the mid-Victorian world where the fine artist or scholar designed – that is to say, developed – ornament which could then be added to any manufactured article. This was the world where a sculptor such as Alfred Stevens was employed to design cast-iron stoves and, inevitably, produced coal-burning monuments.

An eccentric and original figure of the mid-century was the architect William Burges (1827–81) who was employed less than his talents deserved. His passion for medieval metalwork was first revealed while he was working for Sir Matthew Digby Wyatt. His transformation of the interiors at Cardiff Castle for the Marquis of Bute into a polychrome fantasy combines impeccable craftsmanship with a joyful relish for those medieval forms – an 'inhabited' as opposed to an 'archeological' Gothic. These same qualities distinguish his designs for metalwork, such as the elaborate decanter of 1865–66, an antiquarian dream (Fig. 1), or, less congested with visual footnotes, the tableware made for Lord Bute in 1880 (Fig. 8).

In 1861 the commercial firm of Morris and Company was set up. Manifest in the firm's activities is Morris' own definition of art: 'The expression by man of his pleasure in labour'. Morris tried to trans-

form the motives and methods of production itself. For Morris & Co., Philip Webb (1831–1915) designed metalwork in a sturdy, medieval style which echoes the good sense and the control of proportions found in his architecture (Fig. 9).

The man who made Cole's and Digby Wyatt's words work in an industrial context was Christopher Dresser (1834–1904), an almost exact contemporary of Morris. After two teenage years at the Somerset House School of Design he trained, and then lectured, as a botanist. In bringing these two elements together – in relating the structural functions of plants to design – he was conscious of Owen Jones' mastery of pattern. But when he added the third dimension, particularly in his designs for silver and silver plate, he demolished the Victorian assumption that design meant choice of ornament.

Dresser's botanical studies had convinced him that what his contemporaries praised as ornament – the ripples and twists of acanthus, or the looping spirals of honeysuckle – were not decoration, but function expressed as structure. His own design tried to follow this method, with extraordinary results: plain forms made with the absolute minimum of material acknowledge no influence other than function. Dresser's teapots and claret-jugs, their design calculated for grip and balance, made no concessions to Morris' insistence on handwork. His surfaces are industrial metal, straight from the rolling-mill; their even shine reflects the polishing-lathe, not the picturesque dimples of the craftsman's planishing-hammer (Fig. 6).

C. R. Ashbee (1863–1942), whose Guild of Handicraft echoed the Morris tradition of a small society dedicated to non-capitalist principles, did not ban machinery absolutely, but shrank from the mechanical harshness that Dresser accepted. Ashbee probably came nearest to Morris' ideals. He was chief designer, but much of the Guild's work seems to have evolved from work-bench discussion. In silver or silver plate, the softly pounded domes and delicate wires, discreetly decorated and burnished to a dim grey sheen, suggest the Art Nouveau style but lack its ecstatic stress and strain (Figs. 3 and 7).

In 1854 Japan had renewed contact with the outside world, triggering off new fashions across Europe and America. In 1862 the first oriental store was set up in Paris and from the 1870s similar shops appeared in London; one was the Art Furniture Alliance, a short-lived venture organised by Christopher Dresser in the 1880s; this followed his Government-sponsored visit to Japan in 1876. The visit resulted at first in imports and then in the production of imitations of Japanese metalwork. Dresser was thought to be ahead of his time in this appreciation of oriental design.

The interest of Arthur Lasenby Liberty in Dresser's schemes prompted him to become a shareholder in the Bond Street project; in 1877 he had set up his own shop, in Regent Street. The new Liberty shop was an *entrepôt* where the goods presented a glamorous blend of the most adventurous styles. From 1899, Liberty's Cymric silver was produced. Freelance designers were employed: Rex Silver (Fig. 4), Archibald Knox and Jessie M. King (who lent something of C. R. Mackintosh's tough, compact line). These and some other designers' names appear in the Arts and Crafts Exhibition Society's lists; Liberty's own policy for designers was anonymity. In silver or pewter, which

Museum Photo

Aesthetic Metalwork

Fig. 5 **Teapot,** *designed by
C. F. A. Voysey (1857–1941),
c.1896. Brass, machine turned.
(Victoria and Albert Museum.)*

Fig. 6 **Tea-service,** *designed by
Christopher Dresser (1834–1904)
for James Dixon & Sons,
Sheffield, 1880. Electro-plated
nickel silver. This was previously
in the possession of the designer.
(Victoria and Albert Museum.)*

Fig. 7 **Decanter,** *designed by
C. R. Ashbee (1863–1942), the
glass made by James Powell and
Sons, Whitefriars Glassworks,
London, the silver mounts
bearing the mark of the Guild of
Handicraft Ltd., London,
1904–5. The finial is set with a
chrysoprase.
(Victoria and Albert Museum.)*

Fig. 8 **Centrepiece** *of a dessert-
service, designed by William
Burges (1827–81) and made by
Barkentin and Krall, London,
1880–81. Silver and silver gilt
with enamelled decoration and
set with semi-precious stones and
beads. The service was made for
the Marquis of Bute as a wedding
present for his friend George
Edward Sneyd.
(Victoria and Albert Museum.)*

Fig. 9 **Candlestick,** *one of a pair
designed by Philip Webb (1831–
1915), c.1861. Copper.
These handsome Arts and Crafts
candlesticks were made for
Edward Burne-Jones.
(Victoria and Albert Museum.)*

5

Sally Chappell

6

Sally Chappell

7

A. C. Cooper

8

A. C. Cooper

9

A. C. Cooper

was produced as Tudric from 1902, the same general style prevailed. Both Cymric and Tudric ranges assumed a handicraft appearance, although produced in quantity. In form and character some designs were close to the Guild of Handicraft style, but technically there was little contact between designer and maker. Liberty's London silver mark (LY & CO) was registered in 1894; but the Birmingham firm of W. H. Haseler produced the silver from 1901 and subsequently the pewter. Production of some of these early patterns continued into the 1920s.

MUSEUMS AND COLLECTIONS
Although most Arts and Crafts and Aesthetic metalwork is still in private hands, examples may be seen at the following:
GREAT BRITAIN
Birmingham: Birmingham Museum and Art Gallery
Glasgow: Glasgow School of Art
London: Bethnal Green Museum
Leighton House Art Gallery and Museum
Victoria and Albert Museum
William Morris Gallery, Walthamstow
Manchester: City of Manchester Art Galleries

FURTHER READING
Goldsmiths and Silversmiths by Hugh Honour, London, 1971.
Jewelry 1837–1901 by Margaret Flower, London, 1968.
Modern Silver Throughout the World 1880–1967 by Graham Hughes, London, 1967.
Jewellery from the Renaissance to Art Nouveau by Claude Frégnac, translated by D. L. de Lauriston, London, 1965.
Modern Jewelry 1890–1963 by Graham Hughes, London, 1963.
Victorian Silver and Silver Plate by Patricia Wardle, London, 1963.
'The Liberty Metalwork Venture' by Shirley Bury in **Architectural Review**, February 1963.

Malcolm Haslam

Pottery for Aesthetes

R. Todd-White

Fig. 1 **Burmantofts Faience**, c.1880–1904. Left to right: **Vase**, *earthenware with coloured glazes, height 9½ ins.* **Double-gourd vase**, *earthenware with coloured glaze over incised ornament, height 6¾ ins.* **Rose-leaf bowl**, *earthenware with coloured glaze over incised ornament and pierced, height 7 ins.* **Bottle**, *glazed earthenware, height 9¾ ins. (Author's Collection.)*

Fig. 2 **Vase and jug** *designed by Christopher Dresser, Linthorpe Pottery, 1879–82. Earthenware with flowing glazes, the jug with incised ornament, height 11 ins. and 6¾ ins. (Author's Collection.)*

Fig. 3 **Vase**, *Burmantofts Faience, c.1880–1904. Earthenware with a design in copper lustre on an iridescent glaze, height 6¾ ins. (Author's Collection.)*

Fig. 4 **Vase** *designed by Christopher Dresser, Linthorpe Pottery, 1879–82. Earthenware with flowing glaze, height 6 ins. The bold simplicity of this shape was very advanced for its time. (Author's Collection.)*

Old and new potteries catered for the Aesthetes, whose desire was to be surrounded by beautiful and original objects

With more or less understanding of its historical significance, pottery manufacturers responded to the new-found and unwonted aesthetic appreciation which beset the British intelligentsia during the last three decades of the nineteenth century. Established potteries; potteries the output of which had previously been restricted to useful or archi-

reflected the taste for *Japonaiserie*. Pinder, Bourne and Company and W. Brownfield produced jugs suitably adorned with Japanese motifs.

From the early 1870s Minton's produced a steady flow of Japanese-inspired pieces. At their most ordinary these are services transfer-printed and hand-coloured after designs, sometimes by W. S. Coleman, of flowers, butterflies, poultry etc.; sometimes the pottery is entirely hand-painted. But Minton's most sophisticated Japanese wares were finely made with elaborate enamelling, sometimes with raised slip decoration, usually with some gilding and often glazed in a striking turquoise blue. Copeland's, too, made services painted

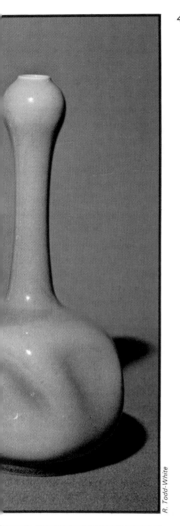

R. Todd-White

4

R. Todd-White

tectural wares; and wholly new potteries, supplied the demand for objects of 'intense' contemplation.

The vogue for Japanese art had particular relevance to ceramics, and modellers and decorators throughout the industry displayed varying degrees of assimilation. The majority reached a stage no further than the adoption of the more obvious shapes and the application of transfer-printed decorative motifs from the applied arts of Japan. A rash of fans, roundels, storks and prunus-blossom appeared on the products of the Five Towns; for a time the willow pattern was hardly seen.

Even Wedgwood's, the bastion of Classicism, brought out, among other Japanese-inspired pieces, the Sparrow and Bamboo service with moulded and transfer-printed decoration, the design for which was registered in April 1879.

Moulded jugs, which had faithfully recorded the popular stylistic revivals of Victorian art using subject-matter such as the Apostles and Silenus, now

or printed with Japanese motifs and also employed the artist W. S. Coleman.

William Stephen Coleman (1829–1904) was a talented artist whose painting on pottery was very popular. He specialised in *Japonaiserie* and slightly boyish female nudes, sometimes combining the two and often creating an atmosphere of coy eroticism to which it is perhaps not unjust to attribute some of his success. He was engaged by Minton's in 1869 and was the inspiration for their Art-Pottery Studio which they established in Kensington Gore, London, in 1871. Here, under the direction of Coleman, male and female students were taught the art of painting on pottery by a group of professional decorators from Minton's factory at Stoke, which also supplied the biscuit pottery. The venture was short lived; Coleman withdrew in 1873 and in 1875 the Studio was burnt down. But the fashion of amateurs painting pottery had been established and soon annual exhibitions began to be held, for instance at the china

K. Hoddle

retailers Howell and James in Regent Street. Contemporary periodicals carried lengthy reviews of these shows, which were judged by Royal Academicians. The amateur-painted plaque or vase has perhaps a stronger flavour of the Aesthetic Movement than other art pottery, evoking as it does so vividly the enthusiasm of the acolyte at the altar of Art.

Other distinguished artists who worked for Minton's at this time were Walter Crane, J. Moyr Smith and E. J. Poynter, who all produced numerous series of designs for tiles, and H. Stacy Marks who specialised in medieval scenes and – need one add – storks.

Maw and Co. of Jackfield produced painted, printed and moulded tiles, some designed by Lewis Day and Walter Crane, which won considerable praise; they also made vases and dishes painted

Fig. 5 **Tile,** *Wortley Faience,*
c.1885. Glazed earthenware,
4 ins. square.
The Japanese motif of the
roundel is typical of art pottery.
(Author's Collection.)

Fig. 6 **Vases,** *Bretby Art Pottery,*
c.1885. Earthenware with flowing
glazes, height (left to right)
7¼ ins., 12½ ins., 6½ ins.
Henry Tooth left the Linthorpe
Pottery where he was manager.to
set up on his own at Woodville,
near Burton-on-Trent. The ware
he produced, with great success,
was called 'Bretby Art Pottery'.
(Author's Collection.)

Fig. 7 **Vase,** *Linthorpe*
Pottery, 1879–90. Glazed
earthenware, slip-painted by
Fred Brown, height 22½ ins.
(Author's Collection.)

Fig. 8 **Vase,** *Royal Lancastrian*
ware, Pilkington Tile and Pottery
Co., early twentieth century.
Glazed earthenware decorated
with copper lustre, height 9 ins.
(Victoria and Albert Museum,
London.)

Fig. 9 ***Design for an entrance hall*** *tiled in Burmantofts Faience, by Maurice B. Adams, from* The Builder, *1880. Engraving. This design shows how ceramics could be used in the Aesthetic interior. Not only do glazed tiles cover the walls, but vases adorn most available ledges.*

FIRE PLACE,   COSEY·CORNER

in ruby lustre, some of which were also designed by Walter Crane.

If painted and printed pottery dominated during the 1870s, the '80s were the decade of pottery decorated mainly with coloured glazes. Initially, success was achieved by the Linthorpe Pottery, which was established just south of Middlesbrough in 1879. Its founders were John Harrison, who owned the site of the Sun Brick Works in Linthorpe, and Dr. Christopher Dresser, the designer. The Sun Brick Works was failing and there was considerable unemployment in the area, so Harrison decided to act on Dresser's suggestion to take over the works and use the brick clay available locally for the manufacture of art pottery. The enterprise was as daring as Dresser's designs.

In his designs for pottery Christopher Dresser found inspiration in primitive cultures

Dresser recommended Henry Tooth, an artist from Ryde in the Isle of Wight, as pottery-manager, although he had had no previous experience of ceramics. He made the journey from Ryde to Middlesbrough via Staffordshire where he learnt the rudiments of pottery. Dresser acted as Art Superintendent for the first three years and ceramic artists were summoned from London and Manchester. Several skilled workmen were brought from the Potteries.

The early Linthorpe wares are distinguished both in their designs which demonstrate the originality of Christopher Dresser, and in their decoration which usually involves two or more differently coloured glazes flowing together. Dresser's shapes were based on originals from an amazing variety of sources. The vase illustrated in Figure 4 is clearly derived from a Japanese model; in the context of European ceramics of the 1880s, its simple geometry was revolutionary. Other designs were based on Egyptian, Greek, Roman, Moorish, Indian, Chinese, Japanese, Peruvian (Fig. 2, right), Mexican and Celtic examples, but they were 'in strict accordance with the principles of decorative Art', according to a prospectus issued by the Company in 1879 and 1881.

The flowing, parti-coloured glazes were derived from Chinese ceramics. Henry Tooth wrote: 'The

10

Sotheby Photo

Sotheby Photo

Fig. 10 **Pair of vases**, *Royal Lancastrian ware, Pilkington Tile and Pottery Co., 1911. Earthenware decorated by Richard Joyce with a design in gold lustre, height 9½ ins. Pilkington's Royal Lancastrian lustreware continued into the 1930s the tradition of combining technical with artistic excellence, which was the aim of the greatest artists of the Aesthetic Movement. (Sotheby's Belgravia, London.)*

wares of Linthorpe present us with all the variety and mingled richness of hue which we perceive in old Chinese wares, and which we value in agate, in onyx, and other beautiful stones . . . all authorities agree in condemning vases which bear strongly coloured decorations, be they landscapes, flowers, figure-subjects or birds – whether on white, blue, or any conspicuous background. . . . The Linthorpe ware was designed to meet a growing demand of the present day; it will be found, in its varied effects, to accord with all forms of art decoration, and to take its part in adding richness and beauty to an apartment without disturbing that general repose which we seek to achieve in our rooms. . . . In short, Linthorpe is an artistic ware which seeks its home in artistic houses'.

The Linthorpe Pottery also produced wares painted with flowers in slip and under-glaze enamels. There are many good examples decorated by Florence Minto and Fred Brown (Fig. 7). The wares were slip-cast, the models being thrown by Edward Thomas Radford.

In 1889 John Harrison found himself in financial difficulties and, with the price of white clay rising at the same time, he was forced to close down the pottery in 1890. Christopher Dresser had ceased to take an active part in running the pottery by 1882 and the same year Henry Tooth had left to start his own pottery at Woodville, near Burton-on-Trent.

Henry Tooth and Company made Bretby Art Pottery from 1883. Tooth's partner in this venture was William Ault, who had worked in the Potteries from his boyhood. At first Bretby ware was decorated with flowing, parti-coloured glazes like Linthorpe; a good *sang-de-bœuf* glaze was particularly sought and achieved. The shapes tended to be less original and diverse than those designed by Dresser for Linthorpe, being more consistently oriental (Fig. 6).

Subsequently a variety of Bretby ware was produced called 'copperette', which was made to resemble hammered copper. Another variety imitated bronze, to which imitation cabochon gems were applied. In the early twentieth century, Clantha ware was made, which had a matt black glaze and was decorated with geometrical patterns reminiscent of the Glasgow Style. Bretby Art Pottery was produced until 1920.

There was apparently some disagreement between Henry Tooth and William Ault in 1886 when the latter left Woodville and established his own pottery at nearby Swadlincote. The wares made here were also decorated with coloured glazes which were ground at the works from his own formulae. As at Woodville, a large variety of vases, bowls, jugs, *jardinières* and pedestals were produced; Ault also made grotesques and toby jugs. In the 1890s he acquired designs from Christopher Dresser which often incorporated animal or grotesque masks. Some Ault vases are painted with butterflies and plants and signed with the initials 'C.J.A.' for Clarissa Ault, William's daughter.

In 1880, Messrs. Wilcock & Company, who were manufacturing architectural ware in terracotta, started producing tiles in a very durable buff earthenware which was fired to a high temperature and covered with a glaze largely composed of feldspar. This ware was called 'Burmantofts Faience' after the suburb of Leeds where the pottery was situated, and it immediately proved a popular decorative material on both the insides and the outsides of houses (Fig. 9). Wilcock & Company also found the body suitable for art pottery and over the next twenty-four years produced a wide range of vases, bowls, *jardinières*, pedestals and dessert-services. A range of figures, mostly derived from Chinese mythology, was also made. Burmantofts lustreware bore designs in copper and silver lustre on deep red and blue grounds (Fig. 3).

The shapes of Burmantofts Faience are derived from oriental or Persian models. The glazes were of four principal colours: *sang de boeuf*, orange-yellow, lime green (Fig. 1) and turquoise. Other colours were used, and different colours were blended on the same piece. Some ware was painted with coloured glazes on trailed slip designs, and incised patterns were used extensively. Among artists working at Burmantofts were Rachel Smith and Esther Ferry, who had previously been employed at Linthorpe.

The Pilkington Tile and Pottery Company was founded in the mid-1890s. William Burton, who had been a chemist at Wedgwood's, and his brother Joseph, were put in charge of the pottery. At first only tiles were made but from 1897 decorative pottery was also produced.

From about 1903 the lustreware for which the pottery is famous, and which became known as 'Royal Lancastrian' in 1913, was produced (Figs. 8 and 10).

Among the artists who worked for Pilkington's were Lewis Day and the architect C. F. A. Voysey, who both supplied designs for tiles; Walter Crane, some of whose designs for lustreware were very successful; Richard Joyce, who joined Pilkington's from Henry Tooth's (Fig. 10); Charles Cundall, who joined the pottery as a boy and later became a distinguished painter; Gordon M. Forsyth, an important influence on modern ceramics; and William Slater Mycock.

Pilkington's Royal Lancastrian pottery was produced well into the 1930s by which time the Aesthetic Movement was buried in the past. The artistic and technical excellence of this ware was a fitting memento of the epoch in which such genuine and successful endeavours had been made to combine the best of art and science.

MUSEUMS AND COLLECTIONS

English art pottery may be seen at the following:
GREAT BRITAIN
Leicester:	Museum and Art Gallery
Liverpool:	Sudley Art Gallery and Museum
London:	Victoria and Albert Museum
Stockton-on-Tees:	Preston Hall Museum

FURTHER READING

Linthorpe Pottery by J. R. A. Le Vine, Middlesbrough, 1970.
'Pilkington's "Royal Lancastrian" Lustre Pottery' by Lynne Thornton in **The Connoisseur**, May 1970.
Victorian Pottery by Hugh Wakefield, London, 1962.
Nineteenth Century English Ceramic Art by J. F. Blacker, London, 1911.
Ceramic Art of Great Britain by L. Jewitt, London, revised second edition, 1883.

Colin Franklin

PRIVATE PRINTING-PRESSES

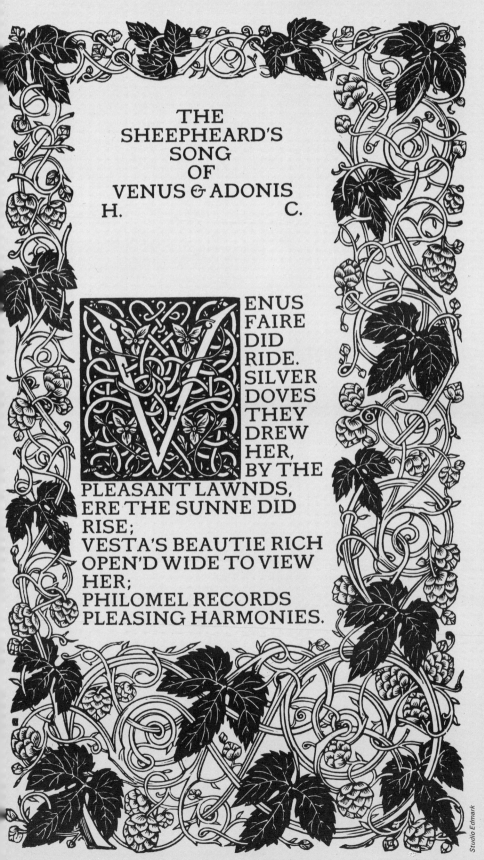

THE
SHEEPHEARD'S
SONG
OF
VENUS & ADONIS
H.   C.

ENUS
FAIRE
DID
RIDE.
SILVER
DOVES
THEY
DREW
HER,
BY THE
PLEASANT LAWNDS,
ERE THE SUNNE DID
RISE;
VESTA'S BEAUTIE RICH
OPEN'D WIDE TO VIEW
HER;
PHILOMEL RECORDS
PLEASING HARMONIES.

Studio Edmark

In an age of mass production and increasing uniformity, the private presses of England began an astonishingly successful campaign for a return to the craftsmanship of the Middle Ages

A movement of protest started with William Morris' first work from the Kelmscott Press in 1891, and it had made itself felt throughout the world of printing before war interrupted its activities in 1914. It seems now to have been an amazing endeavour to protest about decadence in a flourishing, vital industry of late Victorian England and plan to upset it. He did this by returning to the roots of printing-methods, paper-making, ink and the forms of lettering in the pre-Renaissance period he admired and understood.

In that age of uncontrolled pollution and industrial growth, the example of gothic Europe was already important among historians who admired the decoration of early manuscripts, and they had brought a little of its brilliance into their books with the help of scholarship and new techniques of colour-printing. Morris, in accepting the invention of printing, travelled a little ahead of such medievalists as Henry Shaw and Owen Jones.

Morris designed a type based on a fifteenth-century original

The strong belief of these few late Victorian printers was that books should be works over which one man presides in his workshop – as in the days of Gutenberg at Mainz. They argued that if one man sets the type, another in a different place prints, and others design the page and binding or provide illustration, the book cannot have unity. This feeling for singleness in a created thing came from the Arts and Crafts Movement. They also maintained that a man had only to enjoy the work of making to create something beautiful. They said a painted canvas was no more a work of art than a printed book, a chair or a plate. For the Arts and Crafts people, beauty dwelt automatically with pleasure in labour.

After hearing a lecture in 1888 by his friend Emery Walker, and seeing slides of old letter-forms, Morris began to design his own type, basing it on a beautiful Venetian roman letter used by Nicolas Jensen in the 1470s. It was also strikingly like the alphabet of the fifteenth-century manu-

Fig. 1 (Previous page) *The Sheepheard's Song of Venus & Adonis, from the* Vale Press Shakespeare, *published in thirty-nine volumes by the Vale Press between 1900 and 1903. The border and initial were designed by Charles Ricketts as well as the typeface, which he called 'Avon'. After the demise of the Vale Press in 1907, Ricketts threw his types into the Thames rather than let them be debased by less sensitive hands.* (Author's Collection.)

Fig. 2 *Love is Enough, published by William Morris, Kelmscott Press, December 1897. Printed in three colours.* *This masque was written by Morris and published at his press. The large gothic type was also designed by him and known as 'Troy'. Morris designed the Golden and Chaucer typefaces as well.* (Author's Collection.)

Fig. 3 *Paradise Lost, published by T. J. Cobden-Sanderson at the Doves Press, 1902. Printed in two colours.* *The second book of the set,* Paradise Regained, *appeared in 1905. In both books, many of the initials were hand-drawn. The Doves Press, with Kelmscott and Ashendene, are the noble trio of modern private presses.* (Author's Collection.)

Fig. 4 *Christmas carol, from the* Essex House Song Book, *published by the Essex House Press in 1905. Printed in two colours.* *Produced in Chipping Campden, Gloucestershire, for community singing at the Guild of Handicrafts, this fine book contained two hundred songs of England from the Middle Ages onwards.* (Author's Collection.)

2

THE MUSIC.

LOVE IS ENOUGH: cherish life that abideth,
  Lest ye die ere ye know him, and curse and misname him;
    For who knows in what ruin of all hope he hideth,
On what wings of the terror of darkness he rideth?
And what is the joy of man's life that ye blame him
For his bliss grown a sword, and his rest grown a fire?

HE who tremble for death, or the death of desire,
  Pass about the cold winter-tide garden and ponder
    On the rose in his glory amidst of June's fire,
On the languor of noontide that gathered the thunder,
On the morn and its freshness, the eve and its wonder:
Ye may wake it no more, shall Spring come to awaken?

LIVE on, for Love liveth, and earth shall be shaken
  By the wind of his wings on the triumphing morning,
When the dead, & their deeds that die not shall awaken,
And the world's tale shall sound in your trumpet of warning,
And the sun smite the banner called Scorn of the Scorning,
And dead pain ye shall trample, dead fruitless desire,
As ye wend to pluck out the new world from the fire.

48

3

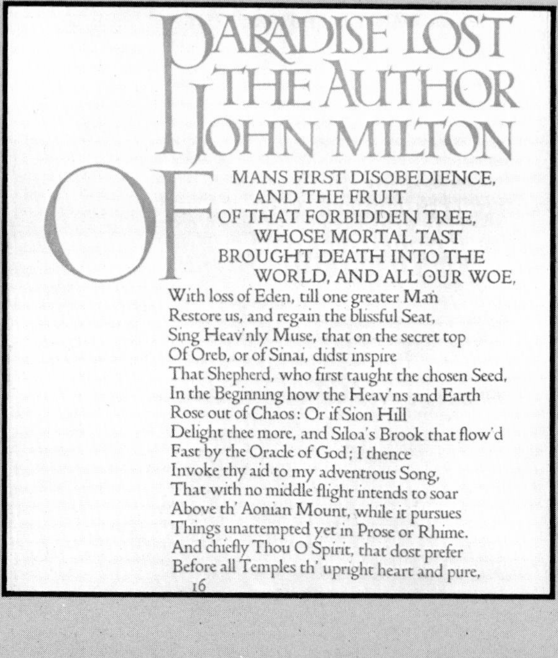

PARADISE LOST
THE AUTHOR
JOHN MILTON

OF MANS FIRST DISOBEDIENCE,
    AND THE FRUIT
  OF THAT FORBIDDEN TREE,
    WHOSE MORTAL TAST
  BROUGHT DEATH INTO THE
    WORLD, AND ALL OUR WOE,
With loss of Eden, till one greater Man
Restore us, and regain the blissful Seat,
Sing Heav'nly Muse, that on the secret top
Of Oreb, or of Sinai, didst inspire
That Shepherd, who first taught the chosen Seed,
In the Beginning how the Heav'ns and Earth
Rose out of Chaos: Or if Sion Hill
Delight thee more, and Siloa's Brook that flow'd
Fast by the Oracle of God; I thence
Invoke thy aid to my adventrous Song,
That with no middle flight intends to soar
Above th' Aonian Mount, while it pursues
Things unattempted yet in Prose or Rhime.
And chiefly Thou O Spirit, that dost prefer
Before all Temples th' upright heart and pure,
16

Studio Edmark

4

CHRISTMAS CAROL.

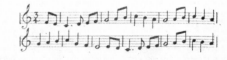

The first Nowell the Angels did say,
Was to certain poor shepherds in fields as they lay,
In fields as they lay keeping their sheep
On a cold winter's night that was so deep.

Chorus. Nowell, Nowell, Nowell, Nowell,
    Born is the King of Israel!

They looked up and saw a star
Shining in the East beyond them far,
And to the earth it gave great light,
And so it continued both day and night.

Chorus. Nowell, Nowell, Nowell, Nowell,
    Born is the King of Israel!

And by the light of that same star
Three wise men came from country far
To seek for a King was their intent,
And to follow the star wherever it went.

Chorus. Nowell, Nowell, Nowell, Nowell,
    Born is the King of Israel!

CHRISTABEL.
PART THE FIRST.

THE MIDDLE OF NIGHT BY THE
CASTLE CLOCK,
AND THE OWLS HAVE AWAK,
ENED THE CROWING COCK,
TU—WHIT!——TU—WHOO!
AND HARK, AGAIN! THE CROW,
ING COCK,
HOW DROWSILY IT CREW.

Fig. 5 *Christabel, published by the Eragny Press, 1904. Printed in two colours.*
Run by Lucien Pissarro, son of the French impressionist painter Camille Pissarro, the Eragny
Press was known for its colour wood-block printing and flawless French neatness of taste.
This example of Pissarro's work is a poem by Coleridge.
(Author's Collection.)

scripts he collected and, in spare hours, imitated.

The need for a privately designed typeface became a characteristic of the private presses. Generally, it would be derived from some admired fifteenth-century printer. Nobody else could use the precious tool. Ricketts, whose Vale Press ran from 1895 to 1907 (Fig. 1), threw his types in the Thames rather than let them be debased by less sensitive hands. His friend Lucien Pissarro designed his own delicate type for use at the Eragny Press and this now lies under the English Channel. The best-known example of this is recorded in the journals of Cobden-Sanderson, whose Doves Press type was furtively lobbed into the Thames night after night by this septuagenarian religious mystic. All were artists, seeking in the books they printed a kind of moral perfection.

Kelmscott, Doves and Ashendene stand out as the noble trio in modern private presses. Morris designed two typefaces, roman and black-letter, and, as two sizes of the black-letter face were needed, they were called Golden, Troy (Fig. 2) and Chaucer after the major works for which they were designed or used. The Chaucer folio, appearing just before he died in 1896, was the *magnum opus* of his press.

A single typeface served the high purpose of Thomas Cobden-Sanderson (1840–1922); once he had invented the Rolls-Royce, which could most dependably carry his cosmic message, he felt no need for a change. It served him as well for the impressive folio Bible in five volumes as for his little duodecimo Credo in a few paragraphs.

St. John Hornby started printing in a summer-house in his father's garden at Ashendene in Hertfordshire in 1895 and closed his press in Chelsea in the mid-1930s. The varied and immaculate Ashendene Press books provide possibly the greatest pleasure and expense for collectors, a few very rare, some of stately splendour, all with the style of a disciple of the Arts and Crafts Movement. As a director of W. H. Smith, Hornby held a position of some power and could apply his ideals in printing and binding commercially.

Independently, and in the tradition of literary privacy, a fellow of Worcester College, Oxford, produced little books of abiding interest for type and content in the last quarter of the nineteenth century. After becoming Provost of his College, he seems to have felt this time-consuming pleasure of his youth could be indulged no more. From the Daniel Press, a family venture shared between parents and their two daughters, we have rare first editions of poems by some of the printer's friends, among them Binyon and Bridges. With friendly help from the University printer, Hart, Henry Daniel brought back into use the excellent types which had been introduced from the Continent to Oxford at a time of poverty for English typography, in the late seventeenth century, by Dean Fell of Christ Church. The Daniel Press, enjoyable to search for now, played its part in the Movement, though Morris and his friends seem to have been unaware of it.

An idea exists that books from the private presses were not really meant to be used and read. They were, of course, but like anything of unrepeatable beauty they should be carefully protected. They were not particularly expensive when new – the Kelmscott Press edition of Keats' poems was issued

6

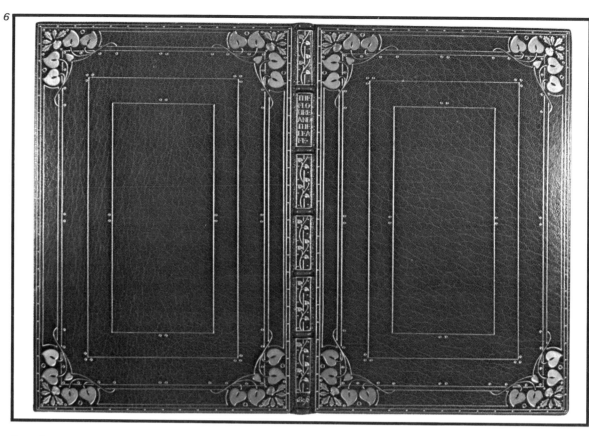

Fig. 6 *The Floure and the Leafe,*
binding from the Doves Bindery,
1896. Leather with gold leaf.
The owner of the Doves Bindery,
T. J. Cobden-Sanderson,
designed for the firm as well as
directing it. William Morris was
keen that all his Kelmscott Press
books should be bound there.
(Author's Collection.)

for thirty shillings. The fairly small numbers printed – in this instance three hundred – were according to demand, taking into account that the scrupulous press-work was reckoned to grow intolerably boring for the printer after a time.

There were other English private presses before 1914 which deserve attention – Vale and Eragny have been only slightly mentioned; the Caradoc Press has points of interest in design and choice of authors, Yeats among them; Ashbee's Guild of Handicraft at Essex House, first in the Mile End Road, Stepney, then in the Cotswolds, ran its own printing-press, and the books are full of lively Guild taste, often very ably produced (Fig. 4).

No single taste governed the policy of the private presses in what they printed. There cannot have been much need for market research with a print run of two or three hundred. Morris printed his own books, Caxton's, and little-edited versions of well-known poets. Cobden-Sanderson's focus always fell upon the mighty example – the Bible, Milton (Fig. 3), Wordsworth, Carlyle and himself. Hornby displayed his cultivated taste in editions of Spenser, Malory, Cervantes, Boccaccio. There are few examples of first editions in the entire output of the English private presses, apart from Daniel's at Oxford, and none of these was important.

This is easy to understand. They had their eyes on eternity, and no new writing seemed obviously safe for that. These were to be great works housed forever as they deserved, examples for future generations. As such, they should be appreciated, and the chance to read Milton according to the vision of Cobden-Sanderson accepted.

Collecting Hints

The collecting of private-press books has become understandably popular. Their influence has led to a new respect for early printing and is present in most new books.

From the first, these books have usually been looked after carefully and one may expect to discover copies in the state which booksellers call 'very fine'. In this of all branches of book-collecting, to buy a second-rate copy cheaply is a poor kind of economy. Avoid, on the whole, the smartly re-bound book.

The books were not necessarily published in small editions, although, as they are absorbed into libraries, fewer circulate each year. Where prices are prohibitive, bear in mind that, by the philosophy of the men who ran the presses, each small task mattered as much as the great finished work; so it is worth searching for the minor pieces – announcements, specimen pages, trial sheets, lists of books published, order forms, printed receipts. These examples of printed ephemera, often preserved, were generally in the book-types of the press and upon fine, hand-made paper.

MUSEUMS AND COLLECTIONS

Printed works from the private presses may be seen at the following:

GREAT BRITAIN

Lechlade, Glos:	Kelmscott Manor
London:	British Museum
	Victoria and Albert Museum
	William Morris Gallery, Walthamstow
Wolverhampton:	Wightwick Manor

FURTHER READING

The Private Press by Roderick Cave, London, 1971.
The Private Presses by Colin Franklin, London, 1969.
A Select Bibliography of the Principal Modern Presses, Public and Private, in Great Britain and Ireland by G. S. Tompkinson, London, 1928.
The Kelmscott Press and William Morris, Master-Craftsman by H. Halliday Sparling, London, 1924.

FRANCE

IN THE SIXTEENTH CENTURY

Lucia Santa Cruz

The Courts of François I and his heirs boasted extravagant and cultured tastes, drawing inspiration from the Courts of renaissance Italy.

Kings of France

François I 1515–47
Henri II 1547–59
François II 1559–60
Charles IX 1560–74
Henri III 1574–89
Henri IV 1589–1610
Louis XIII 1610–43

War was the most important single factor in sixteenth-century France. The strong Italian influence on most branches of French art can easily be accounted for by the Italian Wars and by the French domination of Milan for more than twenty years. The campaigns begun by Charles VIII, and avidly continued by Louis XII and François I, ended in 1559 with the Peace of Cateau-Cambrésis.

When Charles returned from his expedition in 1496 he brought back with him furniture, pictures and rich cloth. He recruited a team of scholars, architects, sculptors, decorators and gardeners to embellish his *château* at Amboise. He was thrilled by Italian gardens and wrote of a garden in Italy, '*Il me semble qui'il ne manque qu'Adam et Eve pour en faire un paradis terrestre*'. Leonardo was also lured to the French Court where he spent his last days, but it was not until François I came to the throne that a conscious and coherent adoption of everything Italian took place.

As is often the case when a nation tries to assimilate instantaneously an idea which originally took many years to develop, French understanding of the Renaissance was superficial. At first they adopted, often in a very clumsy and naïve way, the external aspects of the Italian Renaissance; they fell in love with the way of life at the Italian Courts, their manners, dress and gardens, but failed to understand perfectly the essence of the movement. It was from Italy that the French obtained the intoxicating *joie de vivre*, the love of luxury and sensual pleasures and maybe also the cynicism which seems to have dominated court life in France.

While François was conducting his tortuous diplomacy abroad, important developments were taking place at home. The administration became increasingly concentrated on the *Conseil des Affaires*, which was exclusively dependent on the King, and consequently the monarchy became more autocratic; it could be said that François laid the foundations of absolute monarchy which Louis XIV was to perfect in the following century. The King extended his powers at the expense of the nobility; their rights to administer justice were diminished and the King increased his own domain at the expense of other feudal estates.

While the Italian Wars contributed to the prosperity of those involved in commerce, they ruined the landed aristocracy which could not profit from inflation. The new enriched bourgeoisie entrenched its position in the social structure by obtaining patents of nobility; the *noblesse d'epée* continued to despise the new *noblesse de robe*, but more and more the latter became the depositaries of power.

This centralisation was strongly reflected in social life. The Court became increasingly the centre of all artistic patronage, of learning and of fashion and was the mainspring of every new idea. In an age when the monarchy was so personal, the personality of François greatly contributed to this.

The Ambassador of Marguerite of Austria to France tells us that François was 'as beautiful a Prince as is known to man' and describes François' entrance into Paris after Louis XII's death as a splendid occasion when the King rode 'completely attired in white and silver cloth', followed by great numbers of courtiers sumptuously and extravagantly dressed. From contemporary portraits, which show him in a *pourpoint* of white silk embroidered in pearls and jewels, we can see that he was magnificent, well-built, elegant and truly majestic (Fig. 1).

He was, in Guizot's words a '*brillant enfant gâté*'. He liked tournaments, hunting, danger in all its forms; his contemporaries tell us that he was 'a

2

Fig. 1 (frontispiece) *François I and his Court, sixteenth century. Miniature, $11\frac{1}{4}$ x $7\frac{3}{4}$ ins. François I was, according to contemporary accounts, 'as beautiful a Prince as is known to man'. An aesthete and an avid patron of the arts, his Court was one of the most sophisticated in Europe. (Musée Condé, Chantilly.)*

Fig. 2 *Château of Chambord, begun 1519. Even when François was in the midst of war and threatened with bankruptcy, the building of Chambord continued. By 1539 it was ready to receive the Holy Roman Emperor, who had, in the previous year, signed a truce with France. There he was welcomed by beautiful women dressed as Greek goddesses who threw flowers at his feet.*

Bulloz

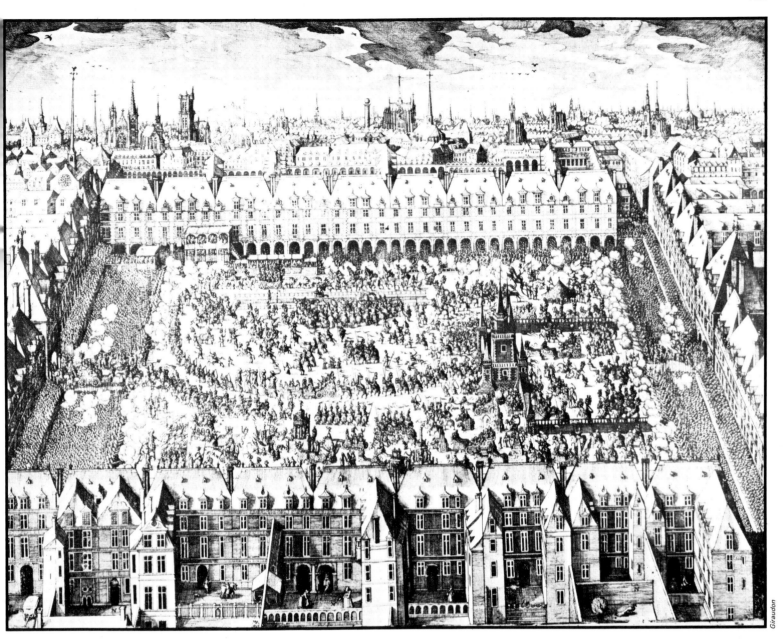

Fig. 3 *Parade at the Place Royale, Paris, 1612. Engraving. The parade took place in celebration of the peace with Spain. In the foreground are depicted scenes from daily life in seventeenth-century France and in the background are buildings of Paris which can still be seen today, such as Notre Dame and the Sainte Chapelle.*

lover of good literature and learned men' and that he tried his hand at Florentine games and verses which he turned out 'with middling facility'. During this time love poetry was pre-eminent and had become practically the philosophy of France. The ascetic virtues of the Middle Ages had given place to a passion for sensual love reflected in voluptuous paintings and verses. François himself loved women; for him 'a court without ladies is like a year without spring, like spring without roses'. His life was to a large extent dominated by feminine influences, above all from his mother Louise of Savoy and his sister, the learned Marguerite. His wife, Queen Claude, the daughter of Louis XII, died young and neglected and his second wife, Eleanor of Spain, suffered a similar fate; but his love affairs with Madame de Châteaubriant and with the Duchesse d'Etampes became legendary.

Fontainebleau, his most loved and intimate residence

Paris was not yet the centre of social or political life. The Court probably spent more time in the Loire Valley than in the Ile de France. As soon as François became king he ordered a new wing to be built at Blois embracing the new concepts of Italian

decoration (Fig. 6). La Fontaine has left us probably the most significant description of it. 'The part built by François I seen from the outside, pleased me more than anything else. There are many little galleries, little windows, little balconies, little ornaments without regularity or order; these make up a whole which is big and rather pleasing'.

The building of Chambord (Fig. 2) was on a larger scale and he continued it passionately even in the midst of war and bankruptcy. It is said that when he was having to melt down silver to pay for the wars and had no money to pay for the ransom of his own children, work continued uninterrupted at Chambord. By 1539 it was fit to receive Charles V, Holy Roman Emperor, who had signed a peace treaty with France. François' most loved and intimate residence was undoubtedly Fontainebleau, built with a very simple exterior and in a far more sober style. The interior was decorated by Rosso and Primaticcio with allegorical and mythological subjects inspired by antiquity. Around these two artists there grew a school later called the Fontainebleau School; it consisted of a group of artists, who adopted the style of these two masters and spread it to all parts of France and to all forms of the decorative arts.

For political reasons and because it seems to have suited royal whim, it was thought necessary for the

4

Bulloz

Fig. 4 ***The Diana of Anet,*** *School of Fontainebleau, before 1554. Stone, height* 60¾ *ins.*
Diane de Poitiers, the mistress of Henri II, was often personified as Diana, goddess of the Hunt and of Chastity. This sculpture, executed for her château *at Anet, has all the attributes of mannerist sculpture; the sophistication of the silhouette, the graceful elongation of the limbs, the* contra-posto *of the forms and the sensual carving of the nude which make this piece one of the most exquisite examples of its kind.* (Louvre, Paris.)

Court to move constantly from one residence to another. It was also essential for hygienic reasons. There was a marked decline of the spirit of cleanliness amongst the French between the Renaissance and the Revolution, and the custom of bathing practically disappeared. In the thirteenth century there had been twenty-six public baths in Paris, but under Louis XIV there were only two. The Sun King himself had only one lavatory in Versailles and that was for his personal use only. Indeed, when Marie de' Medici came to marry Henri IV from the civilised Courts of Italy, she was horrified and made ill by the smell she found at the French Court.

According to contemporary accounts, between January 1530 and October 1531, the Court went to fourteen different places. When the Court moved, everything and everybody went with it: royal wives, children, mistresses, the complete household including doctors, porters, nurses, apothecaries and barbers; in all 15,000 people surrounded the King and they needed 12,000 horses to move. And it must be remembered that the furnishings had become vast and complicated. At Amboise alone there were at one time two hundred and twenty carpets from Persia, Turkey and Syria; forty-five beds, sixty chests, sixty tables; dressers and chairs and a vast number of tapestries from Flanders and Paris. The silver was superb. And to add to the pleasure of life there was a magnificent aviary containing rare and exotic birds. Lions, bears and wild boars were kept and made to fight enormous dogs for the Court's entertainment.

An idea of the size of Mary Stuart's wardrobe can be gained from her accounts. Because she was queen in her own right and betrothed to the Dauphin, François II, we can assume that it was larger and richer than that of other court ladies. There are orders for yards of shot red and yellow taffeta for dresses, dresses of gold damask, dresses of black edged with silver; for canvas and buckram to stiffen the dresses; white Florentine serge stockings, farthingales to hold out the dresses and shot taffeta petticoats lined with red serge.

Of all the women at the Valois Courts, Diane de Poitiers was undoubtedly the most glamorous, the most intelligent and the one who exerted the most

beneficial influence. Her classic beauty, immortalised by Jean de Goujon in his sculpture of Diane the goddess trampling Eros underfoot, is said to have survived the ravages of age. Contrary to popular belief, she was a 'virtuous' widow before her career as *maîtresse en titre* to Henri II began, and the idea that she was also François' mistress is a malevolent legend. She is well known for her patronage of art: she commissioned Philibert de l'Orme to build her a *château* at Anet and discussed the plans with him; she also took an active part in the extensions and the new gardens at Chenonçeau. Her interests were all embracing. As Antonia Fraser tells us: 'She interpreted the role of mistress in the true Renaissance sense rather than in the nineteenth-century style of a grand voluptuary'.

After the death of Henri II, a new period, often designated as the Age of Catherine de' Medici, began. The campaigns in Italy were replaced by far more sinister battles on France's own soil, civil and political disorders which shook the very foundations of the system which François had evolved, and the Reformation was also a disrupting element. The situation was accentuated by the weakness inherent in all regencies when the monarchy is such a personal institution; a collection of sickly children as heirs, with a foreign mother in charge, does nothing to strengthen the political order.

The causes of the Reformation in France were the same as in the rest of Europe: non-resident bishops, pluralism, ignorant and worldly clergy. In its beginnings French Protestantism was 'a spiritual facet of humanism' patronised by François I's beloved sister, Marguerite. It was, however, to the advantage of François to maintain the *status quo* and this is why the monarchy identified itself with Catholicism and indulged in savage persecutions of the Huguenots.

The religious controversy had serious repercussions in the realm of artistic developments. The atmosphere of repression and persecution was by no means conducive to creative thought and to a certain extent it was a negation of the very idea of the Renaissance. On a practical level, the financial consequences of the war meant that private, and above all, royal, building had to slow down.

The political worries do not seem to have affected the continuance of festivities at the Court of the last Valois, however. The work of Antoine Caron is probably the best social chronicle of the time (Fig. 5). His drawings for the Valois tapestries show us the elaborate allegorical court ballets, which were fashionable under Henri III, the *fêtes galantes*, the water parties and picnics which took place while orchestras played in the foreground. The tapestries, *Astrologers studying an Eclipse* and *Augustus and the Sybil* bring out the contemporary delight in anything connected with the occult and they could be a reference to Catherine's patronage of Nostradamus who lived at her Court.

The sixteenth century in France was a period of contradictions; a century which saw the glories of the Italian Renaissance reach its shores, but which also saw the agonising cruelty of civil-religious war. The kings did not apparently find it inconsistent to indulge in severe religious exercises and yet lead comparatively debauched lives. There was refinement in dress and etiquette, yet the most basic elements of hygiene were missing. Above all it created an absolute monarchy which had already sown the seeds of its own destruction.

Fig. 5 **The massacres under the Triumvirate** by Antoine Caron, (c.1520–c.1600).
Caron's paintings are, almost without exception, deeply symbolic. As painter to Catherine de' Medici his work reflects the atmosphere of the Valois Court and this scene from Roman history should be understood as a direct reference to the bloody and violent nature of the Wars of Religion which were being fought at the time that this picture was painted. (Louvre.)

Fig. 6 **The staircase of François I, Château of Blois,** 1515–24. This staircase was built on the site of a medieval tower.

Fig. 7 **A ball at the Valois Court,** French, sixteenth century. The French Court lived luxuriously; there were fêtes galantes, water parties, picnics and elaborate allegorical court ballets. Balls were held regularly, with music, dancing and banqueting. The King's entourage dressed in sumptuous costumes for such occasions. (Musée des Beaux-Arts et d'Archéologie, Rennes.)

FRENCH SIXTEENTH-CENTURY CHATEAUX

The following *châteaux* are open to the public:

1. *Anet* (north of Chartres), open every day from Easter to All Saints' Day (late October), 10–11 and 2.30–6.30.

2. *Fontainebleau*, open every day from 1st April to 30th September, 10–12 and 1–5. Open every day the rest of the year, 11–12 and 1–4.

3. *Amboise*, open every day, 9–12 and 2–7 (or sunset, in winter).

4. *Blois*, open every day, 9–12 and 2–5 or 6, according to season.

5. *Chambord*, open every day from 1st April to 30th September, 9–11.45 and 2–6.30.

6. *Chenonçeau*, open every day from 16th March to 15th September, 9–12 and 2–7. Open every day the rest of the year, closing between 4 and 6.

Fontainebleau

FOUNT OF INSPIRATION

Éditions Chantal (L. Legros)

J. Allan Cash

Fig. 1 **Rostrum of Henri II in the Chapel** by Philibert de l'Orme. It bears a regal inscription and is decorated with Henri's monogram and the crescent of Diana, a curious pagan reference to the King's mistress in a Christian place.

Fig. 2 **Porte Dorée** by Giles le Breton, begun 1528. The three open bays are based on Italian designs but the treatment is completely French. The whole construction is slightly asymmetrical and classical motifs are used in an unclassical way.

Fig. 3 **Gallery of François I** detail by Rosso and Primaticcio, 1530s. The intermingling of stucco (plasterwork) and painting produced an entirely new effect which immediately became popular and was copied throughout Europe.

Scala

When, in 1528, François I decided to convert his medieval hunting-lodge into a sumptuous palace, he gave birth to an artistic school whose name is now equated with the highest achievements in sixteenth-century French art — the School of Fontainebleau. He summoned both French and Italian artists to his Court and there, during the course of the next thirty years, they evolved a brilliantly sophisticated decorative style which deliberately flouted the rules of the classical Renaissance. The forms were elongated, taut and intentionally distorted in an attempt to create emotional and dramatic impact. The virtuosity of the individual artists and the success of the entire project cannot be disputed. The *château* at Fontainebleau is magnificent and takes its place with the Palazzo del Tè in Mantua as one of the finest monuments to International Mannerism.

Fig. 7 **The Nymph of Fontainebleau** by Benvenuto Cellini, 1543–44. Bronze (Louvre, Paris.)

THE ARTISTS INVOLVED

CELLINI, Benvenuto: 1500–71. Florentine goldsmith and sculptor. At Fontainebleau 1537, 1540–45.

DELL'ABBATE, Niccolò: c.1512–71. Modenese painter. At Fontainebleau by 1552 till death.

DE L'ORME, Philibert : 1500/15–70. Born Lyons, trained Rome. Working for Court from 1547.

GILES LE BRETON: French master-mason. Probably chief designer at Fontainebleau from 1528.

PRIMATICCIO, Francesco: 1504/5–70. Trained by Romano. From 1532 regularly at Fontainebleau.

ROSSO, known as 'Fiorentino': 1494–1540. Trained by del Sarto. At Fontainebleau 1530/40.

SERLIO, Sebastiano: 1475–1554. Bolognese architect, trained Rome. At Fontainebleau in advisory capacity.

Fig. 8 **Diane de Poitiers at her toilet,** School of Fontainebleau, mid-sixteenth century. (Basle Museum, Switzerland.)

Éditions Chantal (L. Legros)

Fig. 4 **Design for a window in the French manner** by Sebastiano Serlio from his book **D'Architettura** (1537–51). Serlio's designs had a great influence and were widely imitated by French mannerist architects.

Fig. 5 **Study of a gentleman,** engraving after a drawing by Niccolò dell'Abbate. The *chamarre*, or short coat, often lined with furs, was fashionable and a soft doublet and hose were worn. The codpiece had become increasingly popular. (Bibliothèque Nationale, Paris.)

Fig. 6 **Ballroom of Henri II** by Philibert de l'Orme and Primaticcio, 1540–56. The incongruities of Mannerism are illustrated here. There are vault supports on the piers but no vault. The figures have strangely long limbs but small heads.

Courtauld Institute of Art

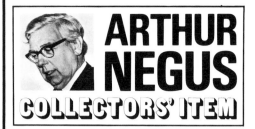

ARTHUR NEGUS
COLLECTORS' ITEM

BANKNOTES

Banknotes were first introduced in England in 1665, although the receipts issued by London traders during the Civil War were accepted as a form of currency. During the eighteenth century a large number of banks issued notes, many of which are valuable today. A ten-pound note issued by the Bank of England in the mid-eighteenth century is worth about £150 now. The Bank Charter Act introduced by Sir Robert Peel in 1844 gave the Bank of England a monopoly for issuing notes within a radius of sixty-five miles from London, and the notes issued soon after the passing of the Act are eagerly sought after today. Victorian notes of £100 and £1,000, of which there are still a large number unredeemed, are worth four or five times their face value today. The *assignats* issued by the Convention during the French Revolution are another form of early paper currency which is easy to find, cheap to buy and beautifully engraved. Banknotes were issued by most European powers during the second half of the nineteenth century. Many of them are of monumental appearance, dark in colour and heavily ornamented with architectural motifs and perspective views. French banknotes were simpler, more colourful and more attractive than most others. The great age of paper money was the decade after the First World War. In Germany, the collapse of the Imperial regime and the rate of inflation led to the introduction of *Notgeld* notes: these emergency notes were very colourful and decorative, produced as they were by local authorities and even individuals.

The stabilisation of currencies put an end to these colourful but almost valueless notes, and with the exception of French and Polish notes, most European banks issued notes of a more subdued and simplified decoration, in keeping with the functional linear designs popular in the inter-war years.

Some collectors make a point of looking for banknotes issued during the Second World War. Money issued to the Allied Armies during the assault on Europe, and to troops in Egypt and the Far East, fetches higher prices than the regular issues of notes. Notes issued by the Vichy Government in France and by the Third Reich itself also arouse considerable historical interest.

Hints To Collectors

Banknotes are extremely vulnerable to wear and tear, and great care should be taken in handling them. They should be displayed in a plastic sleeve, allowing both sides of the note to be seen, or else pressed flat in an album and held firmly in place with a stamp-hinge. Notes with a smooth surface can sometimes be cleaned by rubbing them gently with breadcrumbs, but this isn't advisable for notes printed on a softer paper.

Prices

Prices range between £3,500 for a Bank of England £100 note to £1 for a 1967 ten shilling note. Many of the most attractive notes, German *Notgeld* for example, sell for only a few pence each, and French Revolutionary *assignats* can be bought for as little as £1 or 50 pence.

Top: **French 5000 franc note, 1947,** *typical of the delicacy and colour of all French banknotes. £2.*
Russian five rouble note *issued by the Kerensky Government in 1918, similar in colour and design to the Tsarist notes. 50 pence.*

Below: **American fifty dollar note** *issued in 1854. £2.50.*
German notgeld *typical of the excellent design of many notes issued during the inflation of the early 1920s. 2 pence.*

Opposite: **Polish banknote** *first issued after the foundation of the revived Polish State in 1919. 50 pence.*

Bernard Palissy, the rustic potter

George Savage

Fig. 2 **Bernard Palissy,** an engraving from a contemporary painting in the Hôtel de Cluny.

Fig. 3 **Palissy's signature** from a document; he never signed or marked his pottery in any way.

Fig. 4 **Medallion.** The inscription reads: Faute d'ergent, c'est doleur no paraile (Want of money brings unparalleled misery.) During his earliest experiments, Palissy often made medallions inspired by Roman coins. This one may come from an unsuccessful batch which he broke in despair (it has since been mended), for it bears a reference to his state of extreme poverty at that time.

K. Hoddle

The pottery illustrating this article is attributed to Bernard Palissy (1510–90) or to his sixteenth-century followers.

Fig. 1 **Dish,** decorated with La Fécondité. Although this plate is made of terre jaspée, a pottery process developed by Palissy, the decorative motifs are based quite closely on contemporary metalwork; the subject of Fecundity was a popular one at the time. This elegant design is borrowed from a School of Fontainebleau version and was later copied in London delftware. (Louvre, Paris.)

An eccentric and lonely figure in the history of pottery, Palissy's reptilian fantasies continue to exert today a strange fascination, as does his turbulent and varied life.

Bernard Palissy (1510–90) is one of the first master-potters to achieve a reputation in his own right and to have a distinctive style of pottery named after him. His career was varied and colourful and doubtless exaggerated the reputation founded on his work.

He was born at Agen, in what is now the Préfecture of Lot-et-Garonne and was first apprenticed as a glass-painter. Then, in about 1539, on one of his fairly extensive trips to Flanders and the south German states, he saw a cup which, according to his own words, was of 'terre tournée et esmaillée' (of earth, turned and enamelled) and this inspired him to become a potter. It is difficult to be certain of the nature of the cup to which he refers, or whence it came, but 'turned earth' undoubtedly means pottery and 'esmaillée' suggests that it was covered with tin-enamel of the kind then being made in Italy (maiolica) and in France by Masseot Abaquesne of Rouen who was described at the time as 'esmailleur de terre'. In modern France *émail is still correctly* employed to refer to tin-enamel, the term for a transparent glaze on pottery being *vernis*.

'I set myself to discover enamels like a man who gropes in darkness'.

'Thenceforward', wrote Palissy, 'caring nothing that I had no knowledge of clays, I set myself to discover enamels (glazes) like a man who gropes in darkness'. His search was to last several years and it came to nothing in the end because he never discovered the secret of tin-enamelling. He did, however, discover transparent coloured glazes of extremely fine quality which he used to great effect. But the way was difficult and arduous. On one occasion, to keep his furnaces supplied, he burned first his fence, then his flooring and finally the household furniture, to the horror of his family.

Palissy started without knowledge of the craft he was to master, achieving ultimate success by continual experiment in which he had the services of a practical potter whom he apparently had difficulty in paying. By 1548, the turning-point in his career, he had achieved considerable technical competence, sufficient to attract the attention of the Constable of France, Anne de Montmorency, who had come to Saintes to put down a revolt against the local salt tax. He was given a number of commissions and in 1555 the satisfied patron ordered glazed pottery to decorate a grotto at the *château* of Ecouen, a work which has either disappeared or was never executed.

Palissy made his own advancement difficult by becoming a Huguenot, and in 1562 the local *parlement* accused him of heresy under the edict of Henri II and committed him to prison. De Montmorency procured his release by appointing him 'maker of rustic figurines to the King', which, as a member of the King's household, placed him beyond the jurisdiction of the civil authorities. Soon after this he left Saintes and settled in La Rochelle and then, in 1565, he moved to Paris, where Catherine de' Medici wanted him to make a rustic grotto for the Tuileries, then being built on the site of some old tile-kilns to the designs of Philibert de l'Orme. In this work he was assisted by his two sons, Nicolas and Mathurin, and the three men were described as 'sculptors in clay' and promised 3,000 *livres tournois* (i.e. of Tours) for the work. Catherine created a garden surrounding the Tuileries in a style which had not previously been seen in France and Palissy decorated the grotto with

5

Fig. 5 *Ewer. The design of this piece, like much of Palissy's work, is based on contemporary metalwork. He is believed to have taken direct casts occasionally, but in this piece the work is probably original, as the reclining figure seems to derive from another source. (Private Collection.)*

Connaissance des Arts

serpents, tortoises, toads, frogs and other animals in earthenware covered with coloured glazes. The Tuileries were destroyed by fire just after the Franco-Prussian war of 1870, and only a few fragments of the grotto remain to be seen at the Musée Carnavalet and the Louvre in Paris.

Palissy's work for the Tuileries is, perhaps, that for which he is best known – the '*figuline rustique*' According to a contemporary manuscript, discovered last century by André Potier, Palissy attached pebbles and delicately veined leaves to a sheet of metal to comprise the groundwork and then added reptiles, fishes, and even insects. Over this he poured liquid plaster to form a mould from which the ware was made. This was heated with coloured glazes, described by Palissy as '*esmaux entremeslez en manière de jaspe*' (glazes intermingled in the manner of jasper), and from this the decoration became known as *jaspée*. The effect of intermingled colours can be seen clearly on the reverse of the dishes, where the glaze effect closely resembles the tortoise-shell glazes of Whieldon in eighteenth-century Staffordshire. The manuscript discovered by Monsieur Potier has led to the assumption that Palissy used the bodies of actual animals arranged on his metal plate from which to make casts for his rustic dishes. This, however, is not explicitly stated, and 'modelled animals' is as likely a reading as *nature morte*.

According to Théodore Deck, a nineteenth-century director of the National Porcelain Manufactory at Sèvres, Palissy made no technical advances of consequence. He employed a glaze containing lead, and the oxides from which he obtained his colours were straightforward and well known – blue from cobalt oxide, green from copper oxide, violet from a combination of manganese and cobalt, yellow-brown from manganese oxide and yellow from protoxide of iron; white was produced by using a clear glaze over a white clay. During his lifetime these techniques were fairly generally practised.

It is very difficult to identify his hand with absolute certainty, since nothing was ever marked or signed, and perhaps only those fragments found on the site of the grotto he made for the Tuileries can be regarded as indisputably authentic. His predilection for watery grottoes, and the kind of reptiles associated with them – fishes and lizards, shells, mosses and so forth – has led to the attribution to him of dishes so decorated, as well as cisterns, basins and ewers which resemble the Tuileries fragments in technique and which could have been made as decoration for a grotto.

Swags of fruit overrun with snakes and lizards

Grottoes were a sixteenth-century cult which was at its height from about 1560 to 1570. In 1563 Palissy put forward his own ideas when he published his *Recept Véritable*, written while he was living at La Rochelle, and in 1564 he described the grotto he planned for Catherine de' Medici in his *Devis d'une grotte pour la Royne*. The projected decoration included swags of fruit overrun with snakes and lizards, a kind of vault with cats and birds, and a terrace from which spouts of water fell into a pool in which fish in relief were immersed and to which the moving water gave a semblance of life.

The terrace was further ornamented with corals, ferns, crabs, lobsters and snails. Similar in design are the oval dishes, the *cavetto* representing a stream and the ledge, or *marli*, with modelled snakes and other water-animals. Even this idea was not truly original, however, as grottoes in imitation of water-worn caves had made their appearance in Italy some thirty years before.

Another class of ware associated with Palissy, usually called *terre jaspée*, was based on contemporary metalwork, and in some cases may have been a direct cast. On these the coloured glazes are seen to considerable advantage. Some dishes of this kind were ornamented with figure-subjects, such as the *La Fécondité* which was later copied in London in delftware (Fig. 1). Some work of this kind may have been by more or less contemporary imitators, among whom Claude Bertélémy de Blénod at the Avon potteries (Seine-et-Marne) must be included. The well-known figure called *La Nourrice* was made here – a woman seated with a child on her knees, perhaps better known from the Chelsea Porcelain version of 1750 and often referred to as 'the Palissy nurse' – and it may have been modelled by Guillaume Dupré.

Paris Huguenots were taken from their homes and slaughtered in the streets

Because of his religious beliefs Palissy's life was in grave danger in 1572, the year of the Massacre of St. Bartholomew, when the most prominent Paris Huguenots were dragged from their houses and slaughtered in the streets. Palissy retired to Sédan until 1575, when he judged it safe to return to the capital, and that year he started to lecture on natural history. In 1580 he published a discourse on fountains and ornamental waters, which included an account of his beginnings, difficulties and experiences as a potter. In 1586 the persecution of the Huguenots was renewed and Palissy only escaped execution when a noble patron intervened on his behalf. He was, however, incarcerated in the Bastille de Bucy, where he died in 1590 at the age of eighty.

In the use of coloured glazes Palissy established an alternative tradition to that of the tin-enamel glaze, represented by Italian maiolica. It was continued during the first half of the seventeenth century at Avon, Manerbe (Calvados), Beauvoisis (Oise) and in Paris. It is difficult to separate the products of these centres, however, as problems arise in dating and attribution. Stylistically some can be recognised as decidedly seventeenth-rather than sixteenth-century. During the second half of the seventeenth century, and during the eighteenth, Palissy was almost forgotten, although doubtless his rustic ware featured in some of the *cabinets des curieux* of the period, such as those seen by Dr. Martin Lister during his journey to Paris in 1698, and recorded in his journal. For the rest, the fashionable world turned to faience and porcelain. By about 1840, however, the emergence of the antique collector, taking his place alongside the picture collector in the search for objects from former times, brought a revival of interest in the Renaissance, at first chiefly in Italian maiolica, and then in the sixteenth-century wares of Palissy and Saint-Porchaire. Just before 1850, Minton intro-

6

7

Giraudon

Giraudon

Fig. 6 **Oval plate.** *The almost geometric designs on this plate are somewhat unusual for Palissy, but he was very fond of using these murky colours and tortoise-shell glaze effects. (Musée du Petit Palais, Paris.)*

Fig. 7 **Oval plate,** *of Palissy's 'figuline rustique', or rustic ware type of pottery. It is unusual in that the figures are set on a white ground. (Manufacture Nationale, Sèvres.)*

Fig. 8 **Ewer.** *Grottoes were a sixteenth-century cult; Palissy constructed not only the caves themselves, but also pieces in the same style to decorate them, such as this leaf, shell and snake-covered ewer. (Collection Spitzer.)*

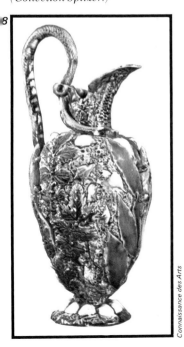

Connaissance des Arts

8

duced the use of coloured glazes into English manufacture under the misnomer of Majolica. Their work of this kind had no resemblance. whatever to maiolica, but technically it was not very different from the wares of Palissy, Avon and the rest, and many of the wares are obviously inspired by him or by his contemporaries. Specimens for copying were procured on loan for the factory by its patron, the Duke of Sutherland. By the year of the Great Exhibition of 1851, Palissy was sharing in the vogue for the Renaissance, and rustic pottery ornamented with snakes and lizards was included among the exhibits. The value of old specimens was rising steeply, and it was about this time that Gustavede Rothschilde paid what was then the relatively large sum of £162 (about £1,500 in today's money) for a dish which had been extensively repaired. The height of the Palissy fever was not reached before the 1880s, however, when a dish was sold for 700 gold guineas (about £6,500 now). Then interest began to wane; fifty years later a reasonably good specimen might have struggled to make £20, and it is only recently that signs of its return to favour have been seen.

The golden age of the Palissy technique was really the nineteenth century. In France a whole school of potters, termed the *Ecole de Tours*, grew up which utilised his techniques. Much of their work was hardly more than an imitation of the old wares, but some, like that of Leon Brard (1830–1902) developed along new lines, such as a combination of coloured glazes with tin-enamel.

The founder of the Ecole de Tours was Charles Avisseau (1795–1860), who began in about 1829 to try to rediscover the secrets of Palissy's glazes. He did not entirely succeed until around 1843, but from 1847 until his death in 1860 his output was relatively large, and gained for him a considerable reputation. Caroline Avisseau, born in 1820, modelled lizards and frogs among rocks in the Palissy manner, and she ornamented small vases similarly. Joseph Landais (1800–83), brother-in-law to Charles Avisseau, was an excellent designer and, like Palissy, a nature-lover. He had considerable influence on the work of the Avisseau *atelier*. Not only did he produce rustic ware of very high quality, but he copied the old dishes, ewers and *tazze* decorated with biblical and mythological subjects which, in Palissy's day, were based on the designs of contemporary metalwork. Léon Brard, who died in 1902, was a pupil of Charles Avisseau. He worked in the tradition of the *atelier*, but with a markedly personal style. These are the principal members of the school, which

operated to within a few years of the First World War.

Of the other imitations of Palissy produced in France it is essential to cite the work of Georges Pull of Paris, whose copies, principally of mythological and biblical scenes, are excellent and deceptive, and are found fairly frequently in the shops of modern French *antiquaires*. He impressed his name into the base of his copies, but this is sometimes covered with what purports to be a collector's label, and any such label on the reverse of what seems to be a Palissy dish is suspect. Industrial and very obvious copies and derivations were made at a number of nineteenth-century French factories – and in Portugal at the factory of Mafra at Caldas da Rainha, founded in 1853. Most of their copies are distinctly crude and not deceptive, but they were capable of better work.

FURTHER READING

Dictionary of European Ceramic Art by W. B. Honey, Vol 2, London, 1953.
La vie de Bernard Palissy by D. Leroux, Paris, 1927.
Pottery and Porcelain by Emil Hannover, Vol 1, London, 1925.
Palissy the Potter by H. Morley, London, 1878.

MUSEUMS AND COLLECTIONS

Pottery made by Bernard Palissy and his followers are on view at the following:

France:	Louvre, Paris
	Manufacture Nationale, Sèvres.
	Musée du Petit Palais, Paris
Great Britain:	Victoria and Albert Museum, London
	Wallace Collection, London

HINTS FOR COLLECTORS

There is little to be said which would help the amateur to recognise the best reproductions and forgeries of Palissy's work in the absence of an acquaintance with genuine specimens. Here are a few pointers about what to expect in a piece of pottery *not* by Palissy:
1. The appearance is too bright and clean.
2. The body is too thick and heavy.
3. The material is often much whiter than that employed either by Palissy or his contemporaries.
4. Marks, such as that of Georges Pull of Paris, are often covered by what purports to be a collector's label; Palissy never marked his work.

EARLY FRENCH FURNITURE

a move towards elegance

Diana Scarisbrick

Fig. 1 *Engraving of the death of Henri II, published in Lyons, 1569–70.*
The magnificence of the carved frame of the bed, the graceful caryatids bearing the canopy and the sophisticated allure of the female form presiding over the headboard exemplify the application of the Fontainebleau court style to woodwork.
(Bibliothèque Nationale, Paris.)

Fig. 2 **Chair.** *This late fifteenth-century throne-chair perpetuates the gothic type of high-backed chest. The medieval structure is combined with renaissance features; triangular pediments, urns and scallop shells illustrate the transitional character of the furniture of the period.*
(Musée des Arts Décoratifs, Paris.)

2

The sixteenth century saw a dramatic change in French furniture. The sturdy, unadorned pieces of the Middle Ages were abandoned in favour of luxurious new styles from Italy. Gilding, painting, carving and rich textiles were lavished on pieces of furniture which were now considered works of art in their own right.

At the end of the fifteenth century furniture in France was medieval in structure and decoration; designed for a feudal, itinerant and constantly warring society – and thus tough, sparse and easily transportable – it was simply carpentry in oak. Yet, by the end of Mazarin's ministry in 1661, French cabinet-makers had mastered marquetry and veneering techniques and were about to assume the greatness in European furniture-making which they maintained until the Revolution.

The event that sparked off this momentous development was the invasion of Italy by Charles VIII in 1495. This attempt to regain the Angevin inheritance was followed by the steady Italianisation of French art, and in the sixteenth century this meant the introduction of the forms and decorative motifs used in classical antiquity. Italianisation also meant the emulation of a particularly sumptuous style of living, a style brought to the centre of French courtly life by Catherine de' Medici in 1533. In the seventeenth century the luxurious tastes of Marie de' Medici, then Anne of Austria, and the great ministers, Cardinals Richelieu and Mazarin, ensured the perpetuation of Italian influences right up to the accession of Louis XIV, though by this time admiration for Flemish art was added to the long-standing dependence on Italy.

The Italianisation of French art coincided with a radical change in the social and political order. The feudal baron was transformed into a courtier and his medieval fortress with its camp-like interior was replaced by a splendid renaissance mansion. This created a need for furniture of a luxurious and fashionable character based on the forms of antique architecture from Italy; furniture became autonomous and an object of value in its own right, worthy of the expense hitherto lavished on textiles.

Yet, in spite of the change in its role and status, furniture remained scarce during this period and had therefore to be easily portable. Until the time of Louis XIV, not even the monarch had each of his palaces furnished, so furniture was subjected to the wear and tear of constant shifting from one room to another as well as from one estate to the next. In addition, styles became obsolete and old-fashioned furniture was quickly banished. Nothing remained of the original furnishings of Chambord when it was presented to the Maréchal de Saxe in 1745 and, when Louis XIV asked for an inventory of the royal furniture, only one piece – a cedarwood *armoire* – survived from the Valois collections.

When interest in this period revived, and no great nineteenth-century collection was considered com-

plete without examples of it, the search for renaissance furniture was extended to fields and farmyards. On one of these forays a dresser, now in the Louvre, was rescued from further duty as a rabbit-hutch. Neglect on this scale has often necessitated extensive restoration, and the combination of the skill of the restorer and the greed of the collector means that the temptation to defraud is often irresistible. The Curator-in-chief at the Louvre has estimated that only between two hundred and three hundred pieces considered to be of the renaissance period would stand up to serious examination. As far as Louis XIII furniture is concerned, all the luxury pieces made in the first half of the century have disappeared and those which have survived because of their solid character represent only the more modest furniture of the period.

For this reason the evidence provided by engravings and inventories is extremely valuable. The inventories of the Constable of Montmorency in 1568, of Catherine de' Medici in 1589, and of Cardinal Mazarin in 1653, minutely describe the furniture of those to whom money was no object.

Response to the Italian example was first expressed in furniture of a hybrid character which

3

K. Hoddle

4

Connaissance des Arts (P. Hinous)

Fig. 3 *Design for a cabinet by J. A. Du Cerceau (c.1520–c.1584), published in France c.1550, illustrating the three essential features of the renaissance style in French furniture. Sculptured, elaborate, architectural, Du Cerceau's objective was the propagation of Italian forms. This engraving shows how carefully he studied the architectural outline of his furniture and also his love for the grotesque and fantastic. (Victoria and Albert Museum, London.)*

Fig. 4 *Buffet or Armoire à Deux Corps, sixteenth century, carved in high relief. This style is associated with the name of Hugues Sambin (1520 c.1600), of Dijon. Much of the effect of this exuberant piece comes from the use of walnut which is admirably suited to carving and when polished, as here, gleams like bronze. The air of luxury is produced by elaborate carving, taking the place of the rich textiles of the medieval period.*

appeared in the early years of the sixteenth century. The medieval chest, throne-chair and sideboard were brought up to date by the addition of decorative motifs of a classical character, such as the pilaster or candelabra, sometimes combined with linenfold carving and gothic tracery. This reflected current practice in architecture, both at Gaillon (1508) and at Blois (1515), where classical ornamentation was applied to traditional forms.

In the next phase of Italianisation, which is associated with the reign of François I (1515–47), all trace of gothic decoration was eliminated and the full range of renaissance ornament was applied to structures that tended to remain conservative, though the growing taste for luxury stimulated improvements in technique. Of these the most important was the introduction of the mitred joint which, hidden in the wood, allowed the covering of entire surfaces with decoration. Before this development the obvious divisions into panels had not permitted continuous design. Carving replaced ironwork as the most prized means of decorating furniture and this resulted in a reduction of the role played by textiles, for these carved pieces in the renaissance style were intended to be displayed and not hidden under fabrics, however rich.

With the increased importance of carving, walnut replaced oak; it was softer, easier to work and its dark gleaming colour resembled the renaissance bronzes and plaquettes that must have suggested subjects for the carver to translate into wood.

Among the pilasters, mouldings and grotesques (decorative motifs used by the Romans and uncovered during the excavations carried out at the time of the Renaissance), stylised flora, fantastic fauna, cartouches, trophies and cornucopiæ (goat's horns laden with flowers, fruit and corn), one of the most typical of the François I period decorative elements was a helmeted, bearded, Hannibalesque warrior, shown in profile and framed in a laurel wreath or medallion.

The rarest woods imported from countries as far away as India

Besides carved furniture of this kind, the royal residence contained pieces painted in bright colours, or in monochrome with details gilded and silvered. These were the result of the collaboration between the carpenter, or *menuisier*, and painter, but following the Italian example there was also furniture made by *marqueteurs*, or workers in marquetry. Two of these, Domenico da Cortona and Bernadino da Brescia, had come to France at the invitation of Charles VIII and remained there for many years. Elaborate examples of marquetry, inlay work and furniture were made from the rarest woods imported from countries as far away as India. It was not until mid-century, in the reigns of Henri II and his heirs, that furniture appeared where the handling of both the decorative motifs and the structure shows a thorough understanding of classical principles, as well as bearing the imprint of that innate sense of elegance and genius for woodwork that is particular to the French.

The credit for this 'coming of age' in furniture as well as in the other decorative arts, belongs to Primaticcio. Collaborating first with Rosso and then at the head of his own team, he transformed the Italianisms of François I into a specifically French style. His authority extended to the applied arts as well as painting, sculpture and architecture, but, although drawings exist in the Louvre of the decoration he planned on the doors of the four great cupboards that were to house the royal collection of rare objects, the great impact of his style and taste in furniture came through the publication in 1550 of Jacques Andronet Du Cerceau's collection of engraved furniture designs.

Extravagant, impossible, fascinating interpretations in the mannerist style

Du Cerceau (c.1520–c.1584) was the first French professional artist to apply himself to furniture design and, just as Primaticcio anticipated Lebrun at Versailles, so Du Cerceau was first in that line of great designers which includes Bérain and Lepautre. His collection of engravings (Figs. 3 and 5) included designs for cabinets, sideboards, pedestals and tables and may have been taken from models in use at the royal palaces. He applied typical Primaticcio features to furniture; opulent swags of fruit and flowers, mannered mythological figures, sphinxes, harpies, exquisitely svelte long-limbed adolescent nymphs of the Parmigianino style, terminals whose shafts are encircled by branching foliage; endless varieties of strap-work, broken triangular and circular pediments replaced the characteristic medallions, helmeted heads, candelabra and grotesques of the preceding period. Du Cerceau justified his tendency to overload his designs with ornament by saying that he was offering the maximum of stimulating ideas in the minimum of space. These extravagant, impossible, fascinating interpretations of the Primaticcio manner were never intended to be copied in toto.

Another source of ornament was provided in 1563 with the publication of Du Cerceau's Libre Contenant Passement de Moresques, offering versions of strap-work and arabesques to furniture-makers and other trades. The success of these engraved patterns, and with it the widespread diffusion of the court style, makes it almost impossible to classify sixteenth-century furniture on a regional basis. Even an architect and designer of the calibre of Hugues Sambin (1520–c.1600), of Dijon, included versions of Du Cerceau's designs in his Livre de la Diversité des Termes, published in 1572, though his grotesque terms entwined with insects and reptiles show an even more esoteric sense of fantasy. Traditionally those pieces of furniture in which the carving is highly charged with dramatic expressiveness are attributed to the Burgundian area and the most spectacular of these to Sambin himself.

Determined that France should be self-sufficient in the luxury arts, Henri IV in 1608 established highly skilled foreign craftsmen in the Louvre workshops and thus set in train the process by which French furniture-making was again subject to cosmopolitan influences. Some of these, like the Swiss Pierre Boulle, founded dynasties whose names recur well into the eighteenth century. Through their influence, French furniture of the finest kind became the province of the ébeniste using marquetry or veneering techniques, rather than the menuisier working in the solid wood.

Outside the court circle the menuisier perpetuated the Henri II style, though its character became more massive. Lathe-turning was introduced for the legs and stretchers of tables and chairs and for the uprights of cupboards and cabinets; baluster and twist types recurred most frequently. Mouldings now assumed great importance, used not only to frame the carvings on panels but taking over the entire decoration of some pieces. They were used in various geometric combinations, such as lozenges enclosing squares or subdivided into triangles, or in relief, making diamond-point decoration.

The changes in social customs that accompanied these developments are reflected in the history of seat furniture. During the Renaissance the throne-chair continued in use (Fig. 2), though brought up to date with grotesques and pilasters, and the folding X pincer chair also survived from the past.

To meet the demands of conversation, and pastimes such as gambling, new types appeared of a less monumental character and easier to move. The chaise à bras evolved with its seat resting on four columns joined together at the base by solid traverses; the arms and back were opened up with the arms sometimes terminating in carved rams' heads. Chairs specifically for women included the caquetoire with a high narrow carved back, trapezoid seat and arms extending outwards; a variation of this revolved on a pivot. The chaise de femme had a low seat and high back, and a chair without arms and with carved or padded back accommodated the farthingale. Clouet's Portrait of Charles IX features a chair covered in velvet held in place by brace studs; but cushions, called carreaux, were the usual means of softening the seats of chairs, benches and stools.

Her literary salon assembled around her bed

During the Louis XIII period chairs became more numerous and around 1636 those with arms were given the definitive title of fauteuils. Those without arms were called chaises. They were made of solid wood, with carving limited to the arm terminals, and had turned legs and stretchers. The markedly sober forms of these chairs were counterbalanced by the general use of fixed upholstery. The use of large-headed brace nails to fix the upholstery provided an element of decoration, as these could be arranged in patterns.

The bed, being the centre of the house round which social life revolved, was the subject of great expenditure. Du Cerceau's engravings show that elaborate caryatids and Sambin herms had replaced the slim colonnettes typical of the gothic period and the bed-head was the subject of a magnificent display of carving (Fig. 1). The habit of receiving visitors in bed, which had encouraged the

5

K. Hoddle

Fig. 5 **Throne-chair.** Du Cerceau's interpretation of this chair is majestic, formal and utterly classical. His dependence on temple architecture and other antique prototypes, in this case a sarcophagus, is coupled with his love of animal forms. A piece as complex as this would never have been carried out but was presumably intended to stimulate the imagination of provincial craftsmen as well as to diffuse Italian forms. (Victoria and Albert Museum.)

Fig. 6 *Buffet. Walnut. The mouldings, panels and drawer fronts of this outstanding piece are carved with motifs taken from the entire repertoire of renaissance ornamental motifs. The lavishness of the carving and the magnificence of the design point to the importance of the buffet as the most prestigious article of sixteenth-century furniture. (Frick Collection, New York.)*

Fig. 7 *Table à l'Italienne. Walnut. This piece is typical of many engraved by Du Cerceau and adopted by Sambin. The top has extending leaves supported by two uprights in the shape of a wide-open fan elaborately carved with caryatids resting in scrolled vases united by a broad stretcher. (Musée des Beaux-Arts, Dijon.)*

development of these luxurious styles, continued in the seventeenth century. Madame de Rambouillet's literary salon assembled around her bed; but by this time the upholsterer had taken over and rich renaissance carving had been replaced by magnificent arrangements of drapes, fringes and tassels.

Although the medieval trestle-table covered with a cloth was used right up till the end of the seventeenth century, the increasing taste for luxury led to the emergence of the fixed table, a monumental affair with a richly carved framework, pillars and feet, worthy of its prominent place in the centre of the room (Fig. 7). So, while chairs tended to get lighter, tables became more impressive and unusually high.

These great carved tables disappeared in the Louis XIII period with the eclipse of carving. The trestle type was in frequent use as well as numerous easily portable small tables of solid wood with turned legs, joined by stretchers of H or X forms. Henri IV saw the advantages of a table fitted with drawers and pigeon-holes for filing his papers and from this beginning the eight-legged bureau emerged in the 1630s.

The buffet, or dresser, is most representative of the great flowering of French *menuiserie* in the reign of Henri II (Figs. 4 and 6). Descended from the medieval sideboard on which plate was displayed, it served the purpose of bookshelf, showcase, larder or wardrobe and was made in several versions. Most admired today are those buffets of markedly architectural character, whose proportions and finely balanced ornament translated into wood the architecture of Philibert de l'Orme.

In the seventeenth century the cabinet was the most coveted piece of furniture and the demand for it stimulated the development of marquetry and veneering.

By 1661 when Cardinal Mazarin died, the French *ébeniste* was technically as accomplished as any in Europe, but no designer had yet emerged to give an unmistakably French character to his craft; this was the achievement of Boulle and Lebrun in the next generation.

FURTHER READING

French Furniture by Jacqueline Viaux, London, 1964.

Furniture by F. J. B. Watson, London, 1956. (Wallace Collection Catalogue with introduction and notes.)

Le Mobilier Français by Guillaume Janneau, Paris, 1955.

Le meuble en France au seizième siècle by E. Bonaffé, Paris, 1887.

Les du Cerceau by H. von Geymueller, Paris, 1887.

MUSEUMS AND COLLECTIONS

Furniture of the François I to Louis XIII period is on view at the following:

France:	Musée des Arts Décoratifs, Paris
Great Britain:	Victoria and Albert Museum, London
U.S.A.:	Frick Collection, New York, Philadelphia Museum of Art

Fig. 1 **Dish painted with Apollo and the Muses** by Martial Courtois, late sixteenth century. Height 16⅜ ins. (Wallace Collection, London.)

J. Freeman

painted enamels of Limoges

Geoffrey Wills

K. Hoddle

The craftsmen of Limoges produced enamelled articles for both religious and secular purposes that have a jewel-like quality, as delightful to our modern eyes as they must have been to their original owners.

Limoges, situated to the south-west of Paris, is famed for its cathedral and as an important centre for the craft of enamelling. From about the twelfth century to the eighteenth century skilled artists produced a variety of objects that have made Limoges internationally recognised.

One of the questions that arise in connexion with Limoges enamels is why they should have been produced in that particular place as the work was executed on metal that was not of local origin.

Fig. 2 **Châsse**, or **casket for holding holy relics**, thirteenth century. Gilt metal enamelled by the champlevé method. (Victoria and Albert Museum, London.)

1196

Fig. 3 **Salt-cellar inset with plaques of Limoges enamel** attributed to Jean II Pénicaud, sixteenth century. Height $9\frac{1}{8}$ ins. The enamel shown on the front of the salt-cellar is of Dives in Torment; it is painted en grisaille. (Wallace Collection.)

Fig. 4 **Eucharistic Dove designed to hold the consecrated Host,** thirteenth century. Champlevé enamel and copper-gilt. (Metropolitan Museum of Art, New York. Cloisters Collection.)

Fig. 5 One of the engravings depicting the Labours of Hercules by Heinrich Aldegrever (1502–58). Used for the enamel paintings on the candlestick shown in Fig. 6. (Schab Gallery, New York.)

Fig. 6 **Enamelled candlestick,** signed I.C., possibly by Jean Court, late sixteenth century. Many of the scenes depicted were not original compositions by the enamellers, but were carefully copied, as on this candlestick, from prints made for this purpose by other artists, mostly German. (See caption to Fig. 5.) (Metropolitan Museum of Art, New York. Gift of Ann Payne Blumenthal, 1939.)

It has been suggested that, as there was a constant movement of pilgrims between Limoges and the Spanish centres of Roncevalles and Compostella, both the metal and a knowledge of the craft may have been brought from Spain.

The effect is reminiscent of stained glass

In the Middle Ages, from some time prior to the year 1150, the enamellers employed the *champlevé* process. Shaped hollows are chiselled in the surfaces of copper or its alloys, brass and bronze. These are filled with powdered pigment and, when heated to the correct temperature, the powder melts and flows to fill the recesses. The coloured areas are then made level with the surrounding metal, which is usually gilded. The effect is reminiscent of stained-glass where the colours are in clearly defined areas divided by narrow contrasting outlines. The colours themselves – the enamels – are composed of glass mixed with metallic oxides and are similar to those used in decorating pottery, porcelain and glass. When melted they fuse with the ceramic and metal surfaces.

The earliest enamellers were doubtless attached to monasteries and abbeys and, although the monks may not have been the actual craftsmen, they would certainly have supervised the output to ensure that it was suitable in every way for church use. By the middle of the twelfth century the link had been broken, and the workshops were lay establishments free from ecclesiastical control. Nonetheless, they continued to produce numerous articles for use in churches, both locally and farther afield.

The range of objects for both secular and lay use was wide. For churches there were crosses; pyxes and ciboria, which held the consecrated bread during the administration of the Sacrament; censers and boats for holding incense; croziers, the shaped tops of staffs borne by bishops and abbots; gemellions, the basins for the liturgical hand-washing at Mass; covers for the Gospels; caskets, known as *châsses* and used for containing holy relics, and candlesticks to ornament and light the altar. All of the foregoing bore likenesses of Christ, the Apostles, saints or scenes from the Testaments. A number of memorial plaques were also made for the tombs of important people.

The bones of saints and similar relics were treated with great reverence and were preserved carefully in caskets upon which considerable artistic skill was lavished. While their contents have mostly disappeared long ago, some of the containers remain and a proportion are decorated with Limoges enamels. The *châsse* in Fig. 2 shows the shape of the majority of them, although they varied in detail.

Perhaps slightly later in date than the *châsse* is the attractive Eucharistic Dove in Fig. 4. The wings are hinged to the body, which was intended for containing the consecrated Host; the body of the bird is chiselled to represent feathers and gilded, and the wings are inset with enamels coloured in green, blue, white and yellow.

Hanging shields enamelled with coats of arms or crests

The range of articles made for use in the home was smaller and examples are not always easily distinguishable from ecclesiastical objects. Such things as caskets, which would have had innumerable daily uses, can seldom be told apart from *châsses*, and candlesticks were to be found on the dining-table as well as the altar. One series of items is unquestionably not connected with the church; small hanging shields enamelled with coats of arms or crests were made to decorate harnesses in the

J. Freeman

Fig. 7 *Virgin and Child* by *Jean de Court, mid-sixteenth century. Height 9¾ ins.*
The composition is derived from Raphael's Madonna di Foligno. *Many enamels were copied from the paintings of well-known contemporary artists.*
(Wallace Collection.)

styles current for short periods.

The Hundred Years' War (1337–1453), which was fought between England and France, completely disrupted the Limoges workshops. When peace came the workshops were slowly re-established and there was a complete change of technique. Instead of using enamel in the *champlevé* manner, a different method was adopted. The products which are known as painted enamels, were painted all over in the same way as oil-paintings; a prepared sheet of copper, slightly convex in section, was coated with a layer of enamel of a chosen colour and using this as a background, the artist painted his picture.

A late Victorian writer on the subject of enamelling of this kind, which was at the time being revived, clearly described the practical difficulties of the process in these words:

'The enamels in their raw state are like lumps of dull-coloured glass, and require to be pounded in a mortar or ground on a slab with a glass muller until they are a coarse powder, and they are then mixed with water and painted on the metal more or less thickly . . . The work is fired in a small (kiln) . . . and is fired many times. Great care and knowledge is here required to realise the ultimate effect of one colour over another, and to see that the enamels are put to the right heat, for too much heat would irretrievably ruin the whole work.'

The metal plates received their initial coating on both front and back so as to balance any strain on the thin copper. If this had not been done they would certainly have lost their shape and after several firings would have become distorted and useless. Furthermore, most of the colours melted at different temperatures so that care had to be taken to ensure that those which flowed easily were applied after the others otherwise they would have 'run' and ruined the work.

The author of the above description was writing of a kiln heated by gas – present day electricity serves the same purpose – but the Limoges craftsmen used wood fuel. They lacked such reliable indicators of heat as thermometers and pyrometers, substituting for them experience and intuition. It is probable that they placed small trial samples into the kiln with the main work and withdrew the former at intervals to check the progress of the firing.

A number of the Limoges painters have been identified, both from written records and from signed examples of their work. Others cannot be named, but their styles are sufficiently distinctive to enable a group of pieces to be assigned to them. One of these is known as the Master of the Orleans Triptych. He is known to have been active between the years 1500 and 1530 and the quality of his craftsmanship, together with his use of designs that were up to date at the time, point to the probability that he enjoyed the patronage of the King, Louis XII, or at least of members of the court circle.

While religious subjects continued to be employed, there was gradually an increased use of secular themes, such as illustrations to the story of Homer's *Aeneid* and other mythological subjects. In most cases these were not original compositions by the enamellers, but were carefully copied from prints made by other artists (Figs. 5 and 6).

A further series of enamels is credited to Monvaerni, the name of one artist, or possibly a

same manner as more modern horse-brasses.

All these articles were costly in terms of time, material and labour, so that their ownership would have been confined to the wealthy. In most instances, following the fashion of the time, their owners' armorial bearings formed part of the ornament and this feature usually serves to differentiate between pieces made for private patrons as opposed to those for the church.

The Limoges enamels have been divided conveniently into categories which enable them to be dated with reasonable accuracy:

First there are the enamelled figures set against a gilded background, the latter being decorated either with a pattern of scrolls or with stars, of *c.*1180–1230.

Secondly there are the figures wholly of metal, either chiselled in the flat surface or applied to it (as in Fig. 2), and with the background enamelled, of *c.* 1230–50.

Thirdly there are the figures that have the lines of their features and the folds of their draperies filled with narrow bands of enamel, of *c.*1250–1350. These dates are only a rough guide and in addition to those noted there were several other distinctive

8

Fig. 8 *Charles IX of France at the age of twenty-three* by *Léonard Limousin* (c.1505–c.1577), 1573.
This portrait, showing a royal figure depicted against a blue ground, is typical of the work of Limousin.
(Private Collection.)

Connaissance des Arts (Miller)

Fig. 9 *One of a pair of candlesticks, decorated with formal designs of birds and flowers, the feet with animal masks,* thirteenth century.
(The Metropolitan Museum of Art, New York.
Cloisters Collection.)

Museum Photo

studio where several painters cultivated a similar style. His, or their, span of activity was from about 1475 to 1500 and a characteristic of the group bearing this attribution is that each enamel is executed on a white background. They exhibit a lack of concern with beauty and a preference for harsh colours, while at the same time they are distinguished by their vigorous draughtmanship.

Of the Limoges artists about whom details are more plentiful, the earliest is Nardon Pénicaud, who lived from about 1470 until 1542 or 1543. German prints were usually his models and although his range of colours was not wide, it is notable for a brilliant finished effect. He enlivened backgrounds and details by placing blobs of transparent colour over pieces of polished silver foil to resemble cabochon gems.

Pénicaud lived at a time when the gothic style was becoming outmoded and the stiff realism associated with it was fading under the influence of more naturalistic forms from Italy; his work is a combination of the two: German and Flemish prints provide the principal subjects, but minor details reveal an acquaintance with the renaissance motifs that were soon to oust the medieval ones.

The new style is particularly noticeable in the borders of plates, dishes and other objects painted with a central medallion. Carefully executed panels are framed in typical curling flat strap-work, with gods and goddesses interspersed with satyrs, female masks and winged cupids (Fig 1).

During the half century following 1530, there were a number of other famous enamellers working in Limoges with the Pénicaud family continuing in the ascendant. Three of them shared the forename Jean, distinguished by later writers as Jean I, Jean II and Jean III. Confusion has been caused by Jean II through signing his work with the initials P.I., which stand for Pénicaud Junior.

Whereas the output of Jean I (active c.1510–40) is in a transitional style similar to that of Nardon Pénicaud, the work of the others reveals no trace of medievalism. The three Jeans popularised painting *en grisaille* (the figures painted in white against a black or dark-coloured background) (Fig. 3). Of them all, Jean III was particularly expert in this manner. He was also noteworthy for the fact that he originated many of his designs and was not content, as were many others, to copy foreign engravings.

Another well-known name is that of Pierre Reymond (died c.1584), a prolific artist, much of whose work was executed *en grisaille*. Contemporary with him was Léonard Limousin (c.1505 to sometime before 1577) who, like Nardon Pénicaud, was a member of a large and talented family. He worked in many styles, but is remembered principally for his portraits. They depict royal and noble personages of the period, mostly shown against a blue background (Fig. 8). Other workshops that continued for several generations include those of the De Court (Fig. 7), Courtois and Laudin families. Pieces are recorded as bearing the signature of Suzanne de Court, and, following the custom of the time, she was probably a widow continuing the business of her late husband, the name being that of the 'firm' rather than of the individual.

From about 1625 the output of enamels continued to be high but quality of both design and finish deteriorated. Then, with the rise of good pottery and the introduction of porcelain, the days of Limoges were numbered and by the eighteenth century production gradually fell until it became confined in the main to small items such as patch-boxes and cane-tops which were painted to resemble chinaware.

Of the Limoges pieces made in the finest period, the fifteenth and sixteenth centuries, most surviving specimens are in museums and only a small proportion is available for collectors. Research and study were pursued actively during Victorian times and again in the 'twenties of the present century.

FURTHER READING

Catalogue of the Painted Enamels of the Renaissance by Philippe Verdier, Baltimore, 1967.
Emaux Limousins champlevés des XII–XIV siècles by M. M. Gautier, Paris, 1950.
Les Emaux Limousins de la fin du XVe siècle (2 vols) by J. J. Marquet de Vasselot, Paris, 1921.

CARE OF ENAMELS

1. Because enamels are made of fused glass, their care is relatively simple. They are best cleaned with warm water and soap, but a soft brush may be useful if there is any stubborn dirt.
2. Take care not to knock enamels, for the surface, especially of those that are old and delicate, can easily be chipped.
3. If any enamel is separating from its base – this usually results from direct contact with either heat or damp – it can be rejoined by dipping the piece into a chemical solution, although this should preferably be left to an expert in restoration. Home remedies such as heating the enamel in an attempt to re-fuse it tend to be disastrous.
4. If in doubt, always consult someone who knows; restorers can usually be found through a reputable antique dealer, but if you have any trouble, the British Antique Dealers' Association is a good source of advice as are the museums.

Chasers in Gold and Silver

Gerald Taylor

Fig. 1 *Design for a hand-mirror by Etienne Delaune (1519–83), 1561. (Ashmolean Museum, Oxford.)*

The gold and silver of France has been widely regarded as unrivalled in magnificence. In the sixteenth century the standard was set for her international reputation for superb workmanship and skill.

France in the sixteenth century was sufficiently rich and dynamic to support many centres producing plate, jewellery and the kindred arts of the lapidary and enameller. Little of the period survives on account of the heavy destruction of plate for political as well as natural reasons, for example at the time of the Revolution and during the Napoleonic era. Even in the sixteenth century much was melted down for financing wars or destroyed during the internal wars of religion.

A very small number of the surviving pieces can be securely dated from inscriptions and *poinçons* (hallmarks) or from inventories and accounts. In the sixteenth century even Paris plate lacked a distinctive mark other than the crowned date-letters and the 'small sun' mark that was introduced in 1580 but soon abandoned, not to be replaced until 1632, when the introduction of a new tax on plate required a third mark stamped by a tax official.

Although Paris was the capital city of an increasingly centralised monarchy and the hub of fashion and quality, its goldsmiths did not eclipse in quantity their provincial counterparts until the following century. In quality, moreover, the sculptor and goldsmith, Cellini (1500–71) considered German craftsmen generally superior.

Dating pieces surviving from the sixteenth century poses many problems. An inscription of dedication may contain a clear date for that event, almost always reliable, but it could have been inscribed at the time of the gift to a recently made piece suitable for the occasion, or put on a piece made shortly afterwards with money given for the purpose; it could even have been copied long afterwards on to a replacement. The Reliquary of St. Ursula in the Treasury of Rheims Cathedral is a good example of the former.

It is a measure of recent advances in stylistic and documentary research that this much-altered object has been identified as the nef made by Raymond Guyonnet in Tours for the ceremonial entry of Anne of Brittany, as wife of Louis XII, into that city on 26 November, 1500; it was paid for in the following January. To it, the Queen had added in 1505 the enamelled figurines of St. Ursula and a representative few of her eleven thousand maidens. Later, the new monarch, Henri III, replaced the Queen's arms with his own and added a simulated scroll when he gave the piece to Rheims Cathedral as his traditional royal gift.

There is an important nef now in the Victoria and Albert Museum (Fig. 4), bearing the

2

Forth Studios

Fig. 2 **Candlestick,** *one of a pair, Paris, 1583/4. Rock crystal and silver-gilt, height 20 ins. The maker's mark is an elephant with the fleur-de-lis above and crescent below. (S. J. Phillips and Son, and R. A. Lee, London.)*

Fig. 3 **Ewer,** *sixteenth century. Onyx, enamelled gold and jewelled. This ewer, with a gold standing cup and cover, was presented by Charles IX to the Archduke Ferdinand. (Kunsthistorisches Museum.)*

Fig. 4 **The Burghley nef** *by Pierre le Flamand, probably 1482. Nautilus shell mounted in silver and parcel-gilt, height 11⅝ ins. (Victoria and Albert Museum, London.)*

Fig. 5 **Clock-salt,** *Paris, c.1532. Silver-gilt, height 13⅜ ins. This is presumably the salt that was once in the possession of Henry VIII. (The Worshipful Company of Goldsmiths, London.)*

Paris date-letter *y*. This probably refers to 1482 (rather than 1505) because the maker's mark can almost certainly be identified with that of Pierre le Flamand, a warden of the Paris Guild in the 1470s and 1480s.

Another Paris piece is the gilt salt, which was preserved in the Jewel House at the Tower of London until it was sold in 1649. It was recently acquired by the Worshipful Company of Goldsmiths (Fig. 5). There used to be a clock in its base and on top, a covered receptacle for salt. Almost contemporary is the gold standing cup and cover, part of a gift made by Charles IX to the Archduke Ferdinand of Austria. This, like Cellini's salt (Fig. 6), is now in the Kunsthistorisches Museum, Vienna.

Stylistically, French plate has particular characteristics. Apart from the normal decline in skills that mark small centres according to their distance from major regional centres, and the tendency for more ambitious individuals to move to areas with better prospects, it is natural that work done in the provinces near the Netherlands, Germany and Spain should sometimes betray influences from these countries.

Even in Italy, the transition from motifs associated with ogival architecture to those derived from classical antiquity was not as clear cut as might be deduced from some writers. In a country proud of having introduced the pointed, or ogive, arch, traditionalist elements retained these forms and decorations well into the seventeenth century. The general trend, from flamboyant gothic beginnings, was for neo-classical elements to be superimposed on gothic forms and gradually, by dissemination from the domestic plate of the Court, for a French version of Italian, Flemish and German styles to dominate domestic plate. Buyers of new church plate were usually content to modify traditional vessels much more slowly, especially in provinces, such as Brittany, where Roman Catholic adherents were stauncher in their reactions against Calvinist and other ideological innovations.

An ostentatious way of consolidating wealth

In addition to the national economic regulators connected with war and trade and those due to more personal affairs and fortunes, short term limitations were imposed on the manufacture of plate. All were connected with minting money to pay troops, all provoked strong reactions within and without the trade and none seem to have stemmed the general tide of prosperity throughout the century.

Before banking was introduced, goldsmiths' work had always been an ostentatious way of consolidating capital from coins. A degree of interchangeability was therefore desirable and so an effort was made to relate the alloys used at the mint and those used by goldsmiths according to urgency in fiscal requirements. At the commencement of the century, the wardens of the craft in Paris were firmly in control of a complex internal system of regulations. They gradually lost authority to what became the *Cour des Monnaies* and were forced in 1584 to give up control of the lapidaries; to lose some rights over the *merciers*, who provided useful retail outlets for their wares; to keep a workshop register; to post a notice in their *boutiques* of the

3

current controlled prices of the various alloys and to provide purchasers with written statements of weight, price and cost of workmanship for each item sold (bills of this kind continued into the eighteenth century).

Casting and chasing in line with sculptural work

Since it is technically necessary for solders to be of lower standard than the metals they join, there was a general tendency to over-solder, a problem which, although common to all countries, was dealt with exceptionally severely in Paris. This penalisation had a direct effect on the character of French plate, encouraging casting and chasing in line with sculptural work in bronze and reducing the amount of soldering. Nevertheless, if examples of handles of Spanish ewers of the time or of English tankards are normally hollow, so are those of French counterparts.

The family connexions of the French rulers with ruling Italian houses were parallel to François I's efforts to civilise uncouth elements at the French Court and in the government. The honours accorded to Leonardo in the years preceding his death outside Amboise and the purchase and acquisition of works of Italian art, ancient and contemporary, were preludes to the employment of Italian designers and craftsmen of many skills at Fontainebleau.

Yet not even Cellini himself, who was established in the Hotel de Nesles in the angle between the *rive gauche* and the city walls, made much impression on the trade as a whole, largely because work for the Court was carried out in segregated workshops and taken straight into private ownership. Even Cellini's famous gold and enamelled salt (Fig. 6) had been modelled in Italy and was only finished in 1545 in Paris to be given away

5

P. Parkinson

Museum Photo

Fig. 6 **Salt** by Benvenuto Cellini
(1500–71), 1540–42.
Height 10¼ ins.
Gold, worked entirely with the
chisel. The main figures
represent Sea and Earth. The
gold figures round the ebony base
represent Night, Day, Dusk and
Dawn and between them the four
winds, which are partly
enamelled. Once François I had
shown his appreciation of it,
Cellini took it home and had
some friends in to dine so as to be
first to use it. It was given by
Charles IX to the Archduke
Ferdinand of Austria in 1570.
(Kunsthistorisches Museum.)

Fig. 7 **Drinking-cup**, Orleans,
mid-sixteenth century. Silver and
parcel-gilt, height 5¼ ins.
Although there are several
English cups like this, the best-
known being the christening cup
of 1587 belonging to the
Worshipful Company of
Goldsmiths, London, there
seem to be no other French
examples. Orleans and Tours
were two principal
centres of goldsmiths.
(Victoria and Albert Museum.)

years later; much of his time, moreover, was spent
on sculpture, rather than on goldsmith's work.
While acknowledgement must of course be made
of Italian influences, too much emphasis must not
be given to them. It is significant that not a single
Paris warden bore an Italian name.

Ornamented with a crowned salamander carrying in its jaws the monarch's motto

The most important, prolific and influential
French designer for plate and jewellery alike was
Du Cerceau, the architect and designer, who was
born c. 1520 in Paris and died in 1585 in Orleans. He
had studied in Rome, copied designs of Agostino
Veneziano, as well as designs in architecture and
sculpture, and was himself copied in Nuremberg.
He produced over one hundred designs for domestic
and church plate and half that number for jewellery.
His concitoyen and contemporary, Etienne Delaune
(1519–83), covered much the same ground with the
exception of architecture (Fig. 1).

A fine example of the mannerist style is to be seen
in the Orleans drinking cup (Fig. 7) and the parcel-
gilt (partly gilded) bowl from the second half of the
century, both in the Victoria and Albert Museum,
have a provincial quality that aligns them with
lesser English plate.

The church plate ascribable to the last quarter of
the century is hard to summarise, consisting as it
does in a medley of pieces, many of them with later
alterations and additions. More important individu-

ally and as a group is the residue of the plate
ordered by Henri III for his newly-founded Order
of the Holy Ghost, partly domestic, partly for the
chapel and partly ceremonial.

The truth is that Cellini's five years in Paris,
even reinforced by the further twenty years that
his two Italian assistants remained active in the
royal service, probably had less impact on French
goldsmiths' work than German or Flemish
immigrants working as journeymen, or the designs
that were imported. Another half century had to
elapse before the personal partnership of Louis XIV
with Charles Lebrun made possible the enforce-
ment of a high standard of design with excellence
of techniques, whether on a grandiose or a minute
scale, that made the French goldsmiths the envy
of the world for more than two centuries afterwards.

FURTHER READING

French Silver, 1450–1825 by Frank Davis,
London, 1970.
Continental Gold and Silver by Gerald Taylor,
London, 1967.
Art in Silver and Gold by Gerald Taylor, London,
1964.
Mediaeval Silver Nefs by Charles Oman,
London, 1963.
Le poinçon de Paris (5 vols.) by Henry Nocq,
Paris, 1926–31.

Colbert
and 'le style Louis XIV'

George Rainbird Ltd.

Raymonde Wickham

Fig. 1 **Cabinet** *from the* Manufacture Royale des Meubles de la Couronne, *mid-seventeenth century.*
This cabinet, with its rich decoration, was given by Louis XIV to Charles II, King of England. It is finely inlaid with an abundance of coloured woods. In the
centre is painted a perspective view of Versailles.
(Collection of the Duke of Buccleuch and Queensberry.)

**Born 1638
Acceded 1643
Regency of Anne of
Austria 1643–61
Died 1715**

Fig. 2 *One of a pair of cabinets from the* Manufacture Royale des Meubles de la Couronne, *seventeenth century. Veneered with ebony and inlaid with* pietre diure.
This royal cabinet, rich in decoration, bears the King's insignia, the double L's, and the fleur-de-lis.
(Collection of the Duke of Northumberland.)

Surrounded by shrewd, ambitious and able administrators such as Mazarin, Colbert, Fouquet and Lebrun, Louis XIV built up a centralised state of remarkable strength and influence and *'le style Louis XIV'* pervaded Europe

The organising genius who moulded taste and invented the court style in the reign of Louis XIV was Jean Baptiste Colbert (1619–83), a man of iron will and fantastic ability (Fig. 7). Colbert entered the service of Mazarin (1602–61) in 1651 and on Mazarin's death succeeded him as Louis

Fig. 3 *Portrait of Louis XIV on horseback by Pierre Mignard (1612–95). Oil on canvas. Mignard, lifelong adversary of Lebrun, the King's chief painter, executed this portrait of Louis as a triumphant warrior being crowned with laurels by an allegorical figure.*
(R. Pinacoteca, Turin.)

XIV's chief minister. His ambition was to strengthen France by the development of all aspects of French national life to which end he founded the academies of Architecture and Science, improved the civil code and patronised literature and all the arts.

Although Colbert is given the palm for originating the system of a centrally controlled workshop devoted to producing all forms of the decorative arts for the furnishing and embellishment of

Versailles, the idea came from Nicolas Fouquet (1615–80), appointed Superintendent of Finance in 1653 to Cardinal Mazarin. He built himself a superb *château* called Vaux-le-Vicomte (Fig. 6), and set up workshops at Maincy to supply everything needed for the palace of his dreams. Here was the germ of the conception of Versailles: '*Ce Versailles anticipé*', as Sainte-Beuve in the nineteenth century was to call it. It is reasonable to suppose that Louis and Colbert, who visited Vaux, were not slow to appreciate the excellence of the scheme and to appropriate it for future use.

The historical period preceding the reign of Louis XIV and the personalities and circumstances of that time were the true creators of '*le style Louis XIV*'. The scarcity of native craftsmen and products after the long period of civil and religious wars in the sixteenth century induced Henri IV, in 1608, to bring Flemish craftsmen to the Louvre. Here began that state patronage of the arts which contributed so dramatically to the development of the decorative arts in France, giving them a preeminence in Europe. Later, Marie de' Medici brought a number of Italian craftsmen to France in order to surround herself with the craftsmanship of her native country and to indulge her personal taste.

In this manner, court taste became based on Italy and the Baroque, for even the Flemish workers were imbued with Italian techniques; they were skilled in the use of marquetry and veneers, elaborate designs in intarsia and the inlay of alien materials such as marble and semi-precious stones, all complex crafts assimilated into the Low Countries from Italy through south Germany.

Louis planned Versailles and his reign around the pivot of '*l'Etat, c'est Moi . . .*'

Richelieu (1585–1642), chief minister to Louis XIII, began the art of collecting, ably followed by Mazarin, Richelieu's recommended successor who remained in power until his death in 1661. To these two prelate statesmen, Louis owed his discerning taste and the desire to live luxuriously. Mazarin had cabinets made for him by Pierre Golle who came from the Low Countries and was skilled in the use of marquetry in tortoise-shell and pewter. This technique was later developed to a high degree of individualistic skill by A-C Boulle when working for Louis XIV, whose taste he so perfectly complemented. The cabinets of Jean Macé, who had entered the service of the Queen Regent after having worked for two years in Middelburg, Zeeland, must also have been known to the young King. These cabinets are veneered in ebony, rich and sombre, the enclosing doors carved in low relief; the manner in which the light catches the dark wood was particularly pleasing to the prevailing taste and so expressive of the baroque style.

The interior decorative style of Versailles owes the same debt to Italy. Panelled walls in sumptuous marbles, elaborately carved, gilt features, the painted ceilings portraying gods and goddesses in flight through space without terrestrial embarrassment. Louis, sculptured in marble, is disguised as a Roman emperor or the God of War.

Why did '*le Roi Soleil*' choose to move his Court and dwelling-place to the country outside Paris?

Mansell Collection

And, most important of all, why did he move the administrative machinery of government to Versailles? It was the carefully planned device of a man who was determined that the appalling disorganisation and fragmentation, resulting from the curiously confused revolution of La Fronde, should not be repeated. Louis realised that the strength of the monarchy must lie in a completely centralised government, within one unit, and represented by one person, the King. He planned Versailles and his reign around the pivot of *'l'Etat c'est Moi'*. Colbert was at hand to put the programme into effect.

With Fouquet's ambitions to succeed Mazarin

who had realised the possibilities of the young painter and appointed him director of the works at Vaux (Fig. 5). Nothing was undertaken at the Gobelins without Lebrun's instruction, and, without doubt, he provided at the same time the designs for practically all the branches of the decorative arts undertaken there. He also acted as chief painter to the King. It was the *Manufacture des Gobelins* providing suitable decoration for the King's palaces which disseminated the style and prestige of France throughout Europe. Its influence cannot be over-estimated.

Another member of the team contributing to the style and prestige of Louis, was that master

4

Fig. 4 **Citizens paying homage to the King and the Regent, his mother,** *engraved by Humbelot, c.1650.*
Louis XIV came to the throne in 1643 at the age of five. His mother, Anne of Austria, acted as regent but the real power lay in the hands of Cardinal Mazarin, on whose death in 1661 Louis assumed control. He was inordinately ambitious, and assumed the position of head of the government, traditionally in the words 'L'Etat, c'est Moi'. His reign saw the golden age of the arts in France but conditions of the working-classes were poor. Here he is shown receiving his subjects as his mother looks on.

disposed of by a sentence of life imprisonment for embezzlement in 1664, the way was clear for the centralised system of workshops at Vaux to be taken over and used for the glorification of the sovereign and the moral and economic ascendancy of France. The factory, still employing the same Flemish workmen, remained at Maincy for three years and was then moved to Gobelins near Paris and established as the *Manufacture Royale des Meubles de la Couronne* (Figs. 1 and 2).

The success of the unit
was due to Lebrun

The organisation of the state-supported unit devoted to the manufacture of all the luxury arts was due to Colbert, now Superintendent of Finance and Buildings, but its success was entirely due to the extraordinary talents of its first director, Charles Lebrun (1619–90). Again it was Fouquet

garden designer of all time, André Lenôtre (1613–1700). He laid out the grounds of Vaux between 1656 and 1661, perfecting the classical style of garden design. Vaux was the inspiration for Versailles, expressing unity of design between house and garden. Magnificent as they are, it must be admitted that the gardens designed by Lenôtre are carried out with a complete disregard for nature. Rather they are conceived in terms of a mathematical problem expressed in landscape. It is significant that he lived in the age of the great mathematical explorers. Lenôtre was the first garden designer after the Moors to realise the importance of water, the use of which became increasingly intricate as time went on. He was natural, simple, lovable and without guile. To the end of his life, he remained a valued and honoured friend of Louis. He designed and laid out many great gardens – including St. James's Park and Kensington Gardens, London – and his influence spread throughout Europe and England.

Fig. 6 *Château of Vaux-le-Vicomte* by Louis Le Vau (1612–70), commissioned in 1657. Vaux-le-Vicomte is undoubtedly Le Vau's masterpiece.

Fig. 7 *Portrait of Colbert* by Lefèvre. Oil on canvas. Jean Baptiste Colbert (1619–83) as Louis XIV's chief minister, was largely responsible for promoting the King in his formation of a completely centralised government. (Versailles.)

Fig. 5 *La Comédie* by Charles Lebrun (1619–90) from the Salon des Muses at Vaux-le-Vicomte, begun 1658.
Lebrun's fresco decoration for Fouquet's residence shows clearly how greatly he was influenced by Roman Baroque. He visited Rome in the early 1640s and the illusionism of painters such as Pietro da Cortona obviously impressed him deeply. Lebrun's ability was recognised by Colbert, who created him Director of the Royal Manufactory at Gobelins. He became chief painter to the King and executed his most important works at Versailles, where he was responsible for the Galerie des Glaces.

The architecture of the age of Louis XIV is for good or bad embodied in Versailles and the work of Jules Hardouin-Mansart (1646-1708). He took the name of his maternal great-uncle, François Mansart, the architect, for reasons of publicity. He had great pretensions and was extremely able, and his own career as an architect was also outstandingly successful. Colbert pushed him into the Academy in 1676, entrusting him with the immense undertaking of Versailles. Saint-Simon says of the completed palace, '*le main d'œuvre est exquis – l'ordonnance nulle*'. The exterior is dull. It fulfils its function, giving an impression of immense classical grandeur and size. Architecturally the best part is probably the Orangery, possibly designed by Lenôtre and carried out by Mansart's pupil, Desgodtetz. For forty years Mansart held his position at Court; an entrepreneur, impudent, audacious, extravagant, his heart was set on a lucrative practice.

The master mind who planned and schemed to make France and Louis XIV great and powerful was Colbert. He launched on far-reaching financial and legal reforms, aimed at order and economy, and carried these through, planning for the country to be enriched by commerce. The success of his programme depended on peace. But Louis embarked on a disastrous policy of conquest, so that his reforms came to nothing. Depressed and worn out by overwork, Colbert died at the age of sixty-four. He was a great statesman, conceiving a practical scheme for making France a mighty power.

The loss of so many examples of the decorative arts of the Louis XIV period is unfortunate. Although it was Louis himself who began the system of inventories in order to prevent the dispersal of crown possessions, most of his pieces have disappeared. Vast amounts of the silver and silver furniture and bronzes went into the melting-pot, and the rest was often so fragile that it has not survived the pressure and strain of time.

ARTHUR NEGUS
COLLECTORS' ITEM

TINS

'But they're only old biscuit tins', exclaimed an uninitiated customer, as he paused to look at a stall in an antique market.

But when you see the examples on this page, it is easy to understand why tin-collecting has recently become a serious and fascinating study. The designs reflect popular taste in art and graphics from mid-Victorian times – Art Nouveau, pre-Raphaelite, Art Deco – and many are beautifully executed. Among the most highly prized by collectors, are Huntley and Palmer and Victory-V tins, designs which have won many awards.

The manufacture of tins began with the mass production of food and the problem of keeping it fresh. The story of Huntley and Palmer's biscuits is a typical and early example of the development of tin-manufacturing. London stage-coaches on their way to and from the West Country used to stop at the Crown Hotel, Reading, opposite the shop of Huntley and Palmer,

where biscuits were sold to passengers. To keep them fresh, Thomas Huntley's brother Joseph, who owned an ironmonger's shop nearby, made airtight tins. These were made laboriously by hand, and it was not until the 1870s that the first tin-printing machine was invented, making possible the manufacture of novelty tins in all shapes, and with colourful designs.

This innovation started the tin-making boom. Bryant and May, who packed their wax vestas in wooden boxes, were among the first to see the advantages of tins, and as early as 1872, Joseph Huntley's company supplied these. Other manufacturers quickly followed. Tin-collecting can be divided into three categories: pictorial, brand-name (Saxa salt, Oxo, etc.) and commemorative. The latter are a fascinating record of royal jubilees, coronations and other historical events.

Prices

These range from £1 to £12. For a rare item, expect to pay up to £25.

Above left: *Early tin,* c.1880. £12.

Below left: *Huntley and Palmer book-tin,* c.1890. £14. *Macfarlane Lang and Co. anvil-tin* with reproductions of Landseer paintings, c.1900. £12.

Above: *Huntley and Palmer sentry-box tin,* c.1910. £10. *Victory-V lozenge-tin* with Chinese figures, c.1890. £8. *Ogden's Redbreast Flake tin,* £4.

Opposite: *Brand and souvenir tins,* approximately life size. Prices from £1.

CORONATION DAY · JUNE 26TH 1902

FRY'S PURE SOLUBLE BREAKFAST COCOA · MADE BY FRY'S

NURSERY OINTMENT "SAFETY" BRAND

SELECTED STEEL PENS BEST QUALITY.

Coronation of KING GEORGE V. AND QUEEN MARY 1911

Urilla C

REGAL LOUD TONE NEEDLES 200 200

MENTHOLYPTUS Dr RUMNEY'S SNUFF

BOURNVILLE COCOA MADE BY Cadbury

PLAYER'S NAVY CUT. CIGARETTES Gold Leaf

OXO IN CUBES BRAND FLUID BEEF

K. Hoddle

Faience: pottery to rival silver

Pietro Raffo

In the early sixteenth century
pottery was being made in France
which was comparable with the
finest Italian Maiolica. By the
eighteenth century even
the tables of the nobility were
graced with these magnificent
and elaborately decorated pieces

In describing French faience (tin-glazed earthen-ware), mention must first be made of the pottery known as St. Porchaire, which superficially resembles faience, but which was produced by a quite different technique. Because the clay was fine-grained and rich in silica, the body remained white after firing and the surface was then decorated with coloured lines, the whole being covered with a transparent lead glaze. This technique of decoration may have involved some kind of printing process. On a broken portion of a St. Porchaire plate in the Victoria and Albert Museum the decorated lines are formed by grooves filled with coloured slip, or semi-fluid clay. Underneath the rim the plate bears an indented mark. The decorative outlines on this ware were sometimes impressed on to the soft clay before firing with a stamping iron, and the colours and occasional moulded ornamentation added later.

St. Porchaire ware was made in elegant shapes and designs, and clearly intended for the nobility

St. Porchaire, otherwise known as Henri II ware, was made in the sixteenth century in the most elegant shapes and designs, often bearing coats of arms, and clearly intended for the nobility (Fig. 6). Its exact origin is a matter for dispute. The historian Filon discovered certain documents at the Castle of Oiron, near Thouars, which he believed, proved that around 1529 some out-

Fig. 1 **Sugar castor,** *Rouen, early eighteenth century. Painted blue and white, this attractive sugar castor is in the manner of Delft.* (*Victoria and Albert Museum, London.*)

Fig. 2 **Ewer,** *Rouen, early eighteenth century. Like the sugar castor in Fig. 1, this ewer is of the Delft type known as* Violette *faience.* (*Victoria and Albert Museum.*)

Fig. 3 **Dish,** *by Antoine Sigalon, Nîmes, c.1580.* (*Victoria and Albert Museum.*)

standing pottery was being made there by the librarian, Bernard, and his assistant, Charpentier, under the personal supervision of the lady of the castle, Countess Helen of Hangest. Filon thought that the style of decoration on the pottery was reminiscent of the tooling of leather in bookbinding (Fig. 6). Most of the known pieces of this ware have been found around Oiron and many bear the arms of noble families of the region. Nevertheless, the pottery is now more generally referred to as St. Porchaire, following the discovery of an inventory in Thouars Castle, dated 1542, in which an entry, referring to two *tazze* made of St. Porchaire clay, was found. Another theory is that the ware originated in the vicinity of Paris. Be this as it may, the existence of this fascinating style of pottery shows that the faience technique had its rivals, even in Renaissance times.

The distinctive feature of faience, as of maiolica and delft, is that the clay body is coated with an opaque white glaze made from oxide of tin, instead of with a transparent lead glaze. Opaque tin glaze was an ancient invention used by Assyrian potters in the ninth century B.C. for covering bricks and wall tiles. The technique was rediscovered in Mesopotamia in the ninth century A.D. and used for decorative plates. From there it spread to Persia and ultimately to Europe via Islamic Spain, where the famous Hispano-Moresque style was developed. From Spain, via Majorca, the ware reached Italy where it came to be known as maiolica. Some examples of the technique may have come into France from Northern Italy, but most of the early infiltration was probably from Spain.

In the fourteenth century the Papal court at Avignon employed artists from both Spain and Italy, and tin-glazed tiles and other pottery of the period have been found in the Papal palace and other buildings in the vicinity. These early pieces were rather thin and grey and somewhat coarsely painted. The colouring, like that on early Italian maiolica, was confined to green and purple.

Towards the end of the fifteenth century in Italy, the technique was first introduced of painting ceramic colours on to a thin glaze which could withstand a high temperature. This led to the develop-

4

5

6

A. C. Cooper

7

8

Connaissance des Arts: Boitier

French Faience

Fig. 4 **Plate**, Lyon, second half of the sixteenth century. The Stile istoriato or historical style of Italian maiolica is repeated on this plate, which shows Paris presenting the golden apple to Venus. (Victoria and Albert Museum.)

Fig. 5 **Basin or table cistern**, Nevers, c.1670. This piece is painted in polychrome with mythological scenes after engravings by Michel Dorigny (1617–66). (Musée de Céramique, Sèvres.)

Fig. 6 **Table Candlestick**, sixteenth century, Saint-Porchaire or Henri II ware. Contrasting coloured slips have been used on this piece which was possibly made for the King. The stamped design is reminiscent of book-binding of the period. (Petit Palais, Paris.)

Fig. 7 **Oval dish**, Nevers, 1589. The front of this dish is reminiscent of late Urbino maiolica. The blue wave decoration became a speciality of Nevers faience. (Louvre, Paris.)

Fig. 8 **Vase and cover**, Rouen, late seventeenth century. Painted in polychrome, this vase has an architectural quality reminiscent of the urns which decorate classical monuments. (Louvre.)

ment of the famous pictorial styles in Italian maiolica. In the sixteenth and seventeenth centuries, French faience craftsmen tended to adopt the style of the Italian potters, some of whom had come into the country to build kilns at Nevers and at Lyons (Fig. 4).

The first great master of French faience was Masséot Abaquesne, who was working at Rouen by 1526 (Fig. 9). He found a ready patron in the Duc de Montmorency, who was a great lover of Italian art. In 1542 Abaquesne designed a pavement for the château of Ecouen. In 1543 he was commissioned to make three hundred and forty-six dozen drug jars for a Rouen chemist. They were probably made in the typical Italian albarello shape.

Another master of French faience, whose work was also essentially Italian in character, was the Huguenot, Antoine Sigalon, born near Nîmes. Although he made mainly tiles and everyday pieces, his reputation stems from his elaborately painted faience (Fig. 3). How he acquired the knowledge to produce this is a mystery, but his ware was equal to the finest Italian maiolica. But for the word Nîmes on authenticated pieces, they could be taken for good examples of Urbino or Castel Durante. Although Abaquesne and Sigalon were undoubtedly leading faience makers, their output was not very great.

In the sixteenth century, important cultural and commercial relations were being established between Italy and France. The Medici and the Sforza families established banks at Lyon. Documentary evidence shows that in 1554, the Genoese potter, Griffo, and later in 1574, two men from Faenza, Giulio Gambini and Domenico Tardessir, petitioned Henri III for the exclusive right to make painted maiolica in the Italian manner, which they claimed to have introduced into France.

Although its existence is proven by documentation, little is known about the nature of early Lyon faience, but there is a plate marked 'Lyon 1582' in the British Museum. The Lyon potters are known to have produced faience blanche which was a style fashionable in Faenza. A fine quality tin glaze was left substantially undecorated except for the central portion.

Their success was so great that Conrado was given French citizenship and raised to the nobility

Nevers was another important centre, the faience craft having been introduced there under the patronage of the Duke Luigi Gonzaga of Mantua, who became Duke of Nivernais in 1565 through his marriage to Henriette de Clèves. He was a great lover of the arts and brought from his native Italy some outstanding craftsmen, in particular Domenico Conrado and his brothers from Albissola near Savona. Their success at Nevers was so great that in 1578 Conrado was granted French citizenship, and in 1604 he was raised to the nobility. Between 1588 and 1590 his brother Augustin was in partnership with Giulio Gambini, the Italian potter from Lyon. The strong influence of Faenza discernible on the early products of Nevers was no doubt due to Gambini's presence and the partnership brought to Nevers the best of the late Urbino pictorial style. This phase lasted well into the seventeenth century, the designs including

biblical and mythological subjects (Fig. 11).

Some large figures were also produced at Nevers in the seventeenth century, probably at the Conrado workshop, where the artist, Daniel Lefebvre, was employed from 1629 to 1649. Some of the large Nevers figures are marked with his initials. Antoine Conrado, son of Domenico Conrado, was made faiencier ordinaire to the King in 1644. The monopoly of the Conrado family lasted until about 1630 when other factories began to make their appearance.

Early Nevers faience has mythological and religious pictures copied from contemporary engravings

Nevers faience was usually painted in the style of Savona maiolica, with mythological and religious scenes copied from contemporary engravings (Fig. 5). The clay and the glaze employed at Nevers were harder than those of Savona, and the firing was done at higher temperatures. The resulting colours were of rather faded tints, the manganese pigments tending to turn pale violet and the green and yellow copper colours to lose their intensity. The Nevers potters dispensed with the use of the coperta, the final protective covering of thin, glassy lead glaze which is normally present on Italian maiolica.

A new technique of painting was introduced at the Conrado factory. The basic tin glaze was rendered blue by the addition of cobalt, and on to this ground designs were painted with a thick, white enamel paste. This is referred to as the Persian style, but it is more likely to have derived from Limoges enamels. In the course of time pseudo-oriental designs succeeded the Italian idiom (Fig. 10). The Nevers potters, like most French faience-makers of the day, copied the pottery imported from Holland, where Chinese porcelain styles were the dominant fashion.

Throughout the eighteenth century Nevers remained one of the great centres of French faience, but it never produced a truly French style. The first great innovators in France worked at Rouen. In 1644 Nicholas Poirel of Rouen, Sieur de Grandval and sometime usher to the Queen, applied for the sole right to make white and painted pottery in Normandy. The short-lived factory of Abaquesne from the previous century had disappeared without a trace, leaving no other potteries in the town, and Poirel readily obtained his monopoly. There are no documents extant concerning Poirel's business prior to the deed of sale of his factory and monopoly to Edmé Poterat in 1647. It appears that Poterat, whose name was to become so famous in the history of ceramics, had been making faience on the premises for some two years. He made use of workmen and equipment from Nevers, and at first produced pieces in the same Italian style. The name of Custode, a family that worked for Conrado at Nevers before setting up on their own, appears among Poterat's list of workmen.

After a time, Poterat adopted a new method of decoration that did not require great skill. This was known as lambrequin or broderie, and is seen at its best on large trays or platters, which were made for actual use, not just for display on dressers.

A ROVEN
1542

Fig. 11 **Vase**, Nevers, early eighteenth century.
*Painted with an Old Testament scene, this plate is
in the colours of the Nevers palette.*
(Victoria and Albert Museum.)

Fig. 9 **Tiled panel** *painted by
Masséot Abaquesne, Rouen,
1542.
This panel clearly shows the
influence of Italian maiolica
from Urbino. It shows Mucius
Scaevola at the Camp of Lars
Porsena.
(Private Collection.)*

Fig. 10 **Wig stand**, *Nevers, late
seventeenth century.
Unusual today, the wig stand was
an everyday object in the
seventeenth century. This one is
painted in blue and white with an
oriental design, particularly
popular at Nevers.
(Victoria and Albert Museum.)*

Their dimensions were given in terms of what they would hold, such as twelve to fifteen chickens, or twenty partridges.

By 1663 the faience industry of Rouen was sufficiently developed to come to the notice of the finance minister, Colbert, who was investigating the state of the industries of the kingdom. He made a proposal 'to encourage and reward the Faiencers of Rouen and the neighbourhood, to stimulate competition among them, to supply them with good designs, and to make them work for the King'. The report shows that Poterat had failed in his attempts to enforce his legal monopoly. The first potter to start up in Rouen independently was Butin, who described himself as a painter and sculptor on faience. When it was seen that Poterat's attempts to remove Butin had failed, five other kilns were set up, all in the St. Sever district.

Edmé Poterat's most able assistant was his eldest son, Louis, who like many potters of the time, was fascinated by the secret of translucent porcelain. While still working for his father, he achieved some success in making it and, in 1673, he obtained a Letter Patent from the King, granting him a thirty-year right to manufacture both porcelain and *Violette* faience, that is, faience painted in blue and other colours after the manner of Delft (Figs. 1 and 2).

At the beginning of the eighteenth century the faience industry entered a new period of prosperity and brilliance. Development was aided by the widespread melting down of silver wares instigated by Louis XIV, and followed by his nobles, in an attempt to save the state from financial ruin. There was a need to display something suitable on the dresser in place of the plate, with the effect that there was an immediate run on all

stocks of pottery. This new demand enabled the Rouen potters to turn from the simpler and more economical decorations to more extravagant and ambitious styles suited to the aristocracy. New shapes were introduced, taken from the silver and gold tableware, and plain blue and white colours gave way to elaborate polychrome and to imitations of the *famille verte* and *famille rose* styles of Chinese porcelain. The best of the Chinese style of Rouen was produced between 1720 and 1750.

In about 1740 Rouen potters began to use rococo shapes and motifs and painted scenes similar to those of Watteau and Boucher. Thirty years later Levavasseur, in an attempt to revive the flagging interest in faience and to compete with the products of Marseilles and Strasbourg, adopted the use of enamel decoration.

MUSEUMS AND COLLECTIONS
French faience may be seen at the following:
FRANCE
Marseilles:	Musée Cantini
Nevers:	Musée Municipal
Paris:	Louvre
Rouen:	Musée des Beaux-Arts

GREAT BRITAIN
Cambridge:	Fitzwilliam Museum
London:	British Museum
	Victoria and Albert Museum
Oxford:	Ashmolean Museum

FURTHER READING
French Faience by J. Giacomotti, London, 1963.
Five Centuries of Italian Maiolica by G. Liverin, London, 1960.
French Faience by A. Lane, London, 1948.
La Faience Française by Y. Brunhammer, Paris, undated.

K. Hoddle

K. Hoddle

THE MASTER-DESIGNERS

Philippa Lewis

The title given to Charles Lebrun (1619–90) was '*Premier peintre du Roy*', particularly apt for the man who created a national style, glorifying the king, Louis XIV, his Court and his government. He was the first to conceive of an interior as a unified design: the painted ceiling, the mouldings, the tapestries, the furniture and the bronzes. He did this first in the Galerie d'Apollon in the Louvre (1661), and then at Versailles, in the Escalier des Ambassadeurs, destroyed in the eighteenth century, and the Galerie des Glaces.

Lebrun was no longer solely dependent on Italian renaissance motifs; he combined them with his own invented devices, each one an allusion to Louis and France; the interlaced L's, the fleurs-de-lis, the cock and, above all, the Apollo's head personifying the Sun God. Louis' victories were evoked by the paintings on the ceilings interspersed with a mass of stuccoed trophies and achievements. Versailles was, for Louis, a symbol of great prestige and power. Working with him, and engaged solely for the benefit of the King and Court, Lebrun employed

Fig. 1 **Design for a ceiling** by J. Lepautre, mid-seventeenth century. Engraved by P. Mariette, who sold these patterns from his studio in Paris. This design shows three alternatives for mouldings to surround the painted centrepiece. (Victoria and Albert Museum, London.)

Fig. 2 **Design for a panel** by Jean Bérain, second half of the seventeenth century. Engraved by I. Dolivar.
These engravings were bought by craftsmen who used the designs on tapestries, Boulle work, ceramics and even lace. (Victoria and Albert Museum.)

Fig. 3 **Designs for sideboards, urns and a candelabra** by J. Bérain, second half of the seventeenth century. Engraved by M. Daigremont. (Victoria and Albert Museum.)

Fig. 4 **Design for a frieze** by J. Lepautre, second half of the seventeenth century. Engraved by Le Blond.
It was obligatory to state on every engraving that it was published 'through the 'Privilege du Roy'. (Victoria and Albert Museum.)

Fig. 5 **Design for a pavilion** by C. Lebrun, mid-seventeenth century. Dedicated to Abundance, this pavilion has the characteristic motifs of the Apollo's head and the interlaced L's. (Victoria and Albert Museum.)

Fig. 6 **Design for a pavilion** by C. Lebrun, mid-seventeenth century. In the same series as the Victory and Abundance pavilions, he included designs for pavilions to Apollo, Thetis, Diana and Ceres. (Victoria and Albert Museum.)

Fig. 7 **Design for the ceiling of the Galerie d'Apollon, Louvre,** by J. Bérain, second half of the seventeenth century. (Victoria and Albert Museum.)

Fig. 8 **Design for a door lintel,** by J. Bérain, second half of the seventeenth century. Engraved by F. Chauveau.
This is one of the many ornaments that he invented especially for the Grande Appartement des Tuileries. (Victoria and Albert Museum.)

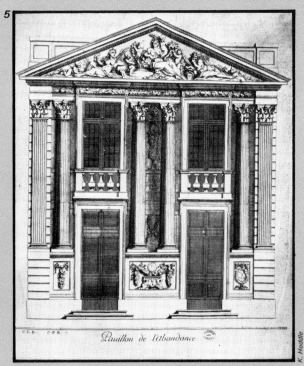

Pauillon de l'Abondance

Pauillon de la Victoire

the most talented and brilliant artists and craftsmen in France.

The foremost interpreter of Lebrun's style was Jean Lepautre (1619–82), who disseminated it among architects and craftsmen in France and abroad with his innumerable richly inventive sets of engraved ornament and design; he included everything from chairs to fountains, ceilings to snuff-boxes.

Important also was Jean Marot (1619–79), whose son, Daniel, (1663–1752) was later to influence England and Holland with his ideas of the Louis XIV style.

The arabesques of Jean Bérain (1639–1711), which were based on both Raphael's in the Vatican and Primaticcio's at Fontainebleau, and his drawings, in a lighter, gayer and more linear style, look forward to the end of Louis' reign and to the emergence of the rococo style. His highly successful designs ranged from a state barge for the King, to the Duc de Chartres' pearl- and diamond-encrusted wedding suit. His patterns can be recognised on contemporary Boulle furniture and silver, tapestry, panels and ceramics.

By 1690, the ebony cabinets and the heavy architectural schemes with their decoration of marble and semi-precious stones introduced by Lebrun were fast disappearing; Bérain used more elegant and exotic, even slightly frivolous, elements, such as *chinoiserie* and *singerie* (patterns using monkeys as the key motif). These characterised the new feeling in interior decoration; a move towards lightness in both design and form and an increased use of looking-glasses, *vernis* (varnishes) and lacquers. His influence was felt long after his death, particularly through the work of his successor, Claude Audran III, a member of the great dynasty of painters and engravers in France during the seventeenth and eighteenth centuries.

Louis XIV died in 1715, having outlived the style which had so particularly been created for him and for Versailles, and which had set off to perfection the magnificent garden of the Sun King.

The first Gobelins tapestries

Madeleine Jarry

Fig. 1 *Harmony or Juno from* The Triumphs of the Gods, *door hangings executed at Gobelins after a cartoon by Claude Audran the Younger, 1699. Wool and silk, 11 ft. 2 ins. x 8 ft. 2 ins. Designed for the Superintendent of Royal Buildings, J. H-Mansart, the subject of this tapestry remains elusive. Peacocks worked into the decorative border suggest that the central figure is Juno but the recurrent use of musical instruments in the design would suggest that she also represents Music or Harmony. (Mobilier National, Paris.)*

Fig. 2 *Louis XIV visiting the Gobelins, one of the series* The History of the King *woven in the workshop of Jean Jans the Younger, 1673–80, after a cartoon by Charles Lebrun. Wool, silk and gold, 23 ft. x 16 ft. 8 ins.* The History of the King *was dedicated to the glorification of Louis XIV (Mobilier National.)*

Fig. 3 *Musical Instruments, detail from the border of* The Seasons, *Gobelins, seventeenth century. (Mobilier National.)*

Giraudon

Organised by the painter Lebrun, the Gobelins workshops flourished throughout the reign of Louis XIV. Founded chiefly to produce tapestries for the glorification of their king, their work was copied all over Europe during the seventeenth and eighteenth centuries

The Gobelins workshops were the creation of Louis XIV. Continuing the policy of his forbears, Henri IV and Louis XIII, he decided to organise in a royal manufactory the tapestry *ateliers* of Paris in such a way that the tapestries woven there would enhance his prestige.

The emigration of the most able weavers from Flanders to foreign countries dominates the history of tapestry in the seventeenth century. The civil wars and religious persecutions, which left Flanders in ruins from the second half of the sixteenth century, created an unfavourable climate for the luxury industries which had been so prosperous in the preceding era. The Flemish weavers gathered in the foreign courts of Mantua, Munich and Nancy, and there exercised their skill.

Even more important was the arrival in Paris, by order of Henri IV, of François de la Planche of Oudenarde and Marc de Comans of Antwerp. In 1602 they installed themselves at Saint Marcel on the bank of the river Bièvre, in the area made famous since the end of the Middle Ages by the master dyers, the Gobelins brothers.

In 1607 Letters Patent gave them numerous privileges among which were titles of nobility and the right to the exclusive sale of tapestries in France. They also received the right to open breweries – the Flemish were great lovers of beer.

The year 1662 is an outstanding date in the history of the French decorative arts. It was the year of the foundation of the *Manufacture Royale des Gobelins* which produced, for more than three centuries, the magnificent tapestries which have made famous the name Gobelins. From the beginning, the manufactory acquired great renown to the extent that there is still a tendency to call all tapestry Gobelins without concern for their date of manufacture or the workshops from which they came.

In an old mansion, Colbert brought together high- and low-warp workshops which had been scattered in various quarters of Paris. He wanted the new manufactory to be especially designed for the use for which he intended it.

With this aim in mind, he undertook such extensive rebuilding that the new installation took several years to complete. The Letters Patent constituting the factory which received the title of the *Manufacture Royale des Meubles de la Couronne*, were granted in November 1667. Between 1662 and 1667 the original project was greatly extended. Instead of only protecting the work of high- and low-warp looms, the *Manufacture Royale* was required to furnish completely the royal palaces; that is to say, as well as weavers, there

were cabinet makers, goldsmiths, mosaicists and many other craftsmen working for the palaces of Louis XIV and, in particular, for the improvement of Versailles.

The Letters Patent of 1667 laid down in detail the internal organisation of the workshops. The workers of the *Manufacture Royale* were accorded the same privileges and exemptions as had been granted by Henri IV to the Flemish in Paris. Sixty apprentices were taken on in different workshops; after six years of study and four years of service for their director, they received the title of Master. The workmen lodged with their families in the outbuildings of the mansion or in surrounding houses, thus forming in this isolated neighbourhood a close community. The edict of 1667 concluded with an absolute prohibition on the import of foreign tapestry under penalty of confiscation and fine. The mode of payment adopted under Henri IV was retained. The directors of the workshops worked for themselves and the King paid for the tapestries according to a tariff settled in advance. The principal materials, silk, wool, gold and silver thread called 'les étoffes' were supplied by the King. A dyeing laboratory directed by the Flemish Josse van den Kerchove was attached to the workshops exclusively for the dyeing of wool. Otherwise the weavers were free to accept individual orders.

With prodigious activity, Lebrun took French art in hand and devoted it to the glory of Louis XIV

The first looms founded at the Gobelins in 1662 were four in number, three high-warp and one low. In charge of the first workshop was Jean Jans from Bruges or Oudenarde, who was succeeded by his son in 1668. The four workshops employed about two hundred and fifty workmen not counting the apprentices. Their director was Charles Lebrun (1619–90) who, with prodigious activity, took French art in hand and devoted it entirely to the glorification of Louis XIV.

Charles Lebrun had been a pupil of Simon Vouet and had spent three years in Italy. Upon his return to Paris, his exceptional qualities caused him to be chosen by the Superintendent of Finance, Nicolas Fouquet, for the fitting out of his *château*, Vaux-le-Vicomte. After Fouquet's disgrace, he worked for Louis XIV and influenced the arts in every sphere.

Lebrun assembled painters who produced 'cartoons' for the tapestries; fifty of them are known including Baudrin Yvart who had already worked with him at Maincy, Louis Licherie, Verdier, Testelin, Houasse, de Sève, Monnoyer, the Coypels, the Boullonghes, Poerson and so forth, each one having his own particular field or talent. They were divided into groups each with its own leader, some painting architecture, others ornamentation or landscape.

Lebrun's paintings, however, were to a certain extent changed when they were transposed on to tapestry by the strict rendering of the different planes and above all by simplification. The tapestries have a classical look, different from the feeling of baroque paintings. The Gobelins models or cartoons were oil paintings which had been fully completed and were cut in sufficiently narrow

Fig. 4 **Mars,** *door hanging after a cartoon by Charles Lebrun, Gobelins, eighteenth century. Wool and silk. 12 ft. 5 ins. x 8 ft. 2 ins. (Mobilier National.)*

Fig. 5 **Interview between Philip IV of Spain and Louis XIV on l'Ile des Faisans,** *detail from one of the series* The History of the King, *Gobelins, seventeenth century.*
The magnificent History of the King *was not only designed by Lebrun; he also supervised the weaving until his death in 1690. (Mobilier National.)*

strips to enable them to be handled easily. A literal copy was demanded. In spite of the firmness of discipline established, however, Lebrun did not attempt to confine the weavers to the exact details of his pictures, but left them to use their normal methods of translation and their primitive range of dyes. He only demanded that the original design should be well respected.

Following Fouquet's disgrace and imprisonment for embezzlement, the King removed the looms and weavers from the workshops at Maincy. The finished tapestries suffered the same fate and were put in the royal warehouse. The first work given to the Gobelins was to finish those tapestries which were incomplete.

A set of *The Elements* and one of *The Seasons* (Fig. 3) were among the initial works given as a model by the first painter at the Royal Manufactory. Next there was *Children Playing in the Garden*, a tapestry repeating the celebrated theme of children's games, so often represented in the sixteenth century by the Flemish weavers. In all these works is maintained an even composition of people and accessories set against a background of greenery, in the purest tradition of tapestry and without any visual tricks. The most famous tapestry by Lebrun is without doubt that of *The History of the King* ordered by the monarch himself, as a record of his personal government, and in the tradition already followed by other sovereigns (Figs 5 and 8). From 1663 to 1673, fourteen pictures were painted retracing the golden period of his reign. Conceived as an apotheosis of the Sun King, this tapestry is one of the most successful works of classical art; whether depicting a scene of battle or of domestic life, it shows the same freedom of imagination and fullness of execution. The colours are magnificently displayed.

The principal associate of Lebrun for this series was the Flemish painter, Van der Meulen (1632–1690), who has left numerous preparatory drawings and watercolours of views of towns, countryside and battles which are still kept at the Gobelins. Lebrun not only painted the models of *The History of the King* himself, but even supervised the weaving until his death in 1690. The first tapestries of the series were woven with one hundred and twenty colours, chosen, registered and ordered by Colbert.

In contrast, the tapestry of *The Months and Royal Palaces* represents the King's recreations. In renewing the theme of the twelve months, Lebrun achieved a great deal of charm. The tapestries most suited to his temperament, however, are without doubt *The History of Alexander*. As a painter of battles, Lebrun showed himself to have been the worthy successor to the painter Jules Romain, pupil of Raphael. During a session of *L'Académie*, the painter Sébastien Bourdon (1616–71) said that one can only admire the extreme ability with which Lebrun treated his crowds, and played with light to 'form groups and to separate one from another'. Though in apparent confusion, these scenes retain a great clarity of narration.

The Gobelins went through a crisis from 1683 to 1694 which resulted in a change of style in the tapestries at the beginning of the eighteenth century. The origin is found in the rivalry of the two painters, Lebrun and Mignard, both *protégés* of two Ministers, themselves rivals,

Fig. 6 *Indian on Horseback* from the series The Ancient Indians *after a cartoon by Albert Eckhout, from the low-warp loom of de la Croix, Gobelins, completed 1689. Wool and silk, 17 ft. 9 ins. x 12 ft. 2 ins. Eckhout, a Dutchman working at the Gobelins, had travelled to the Indies with the Dutch East India Company. (Mobilier National.)*

Fig. 7 *Louis XIV and Colbert at the Gobelins Tapestry Works* by Sebastien Leclerc, seventeenth century. Engraving, $4\frac{3}{4}$ ins. x $8\frac{3}{4}$ ins. Colbert, Controller General of Finance for Louis XIV, was largely responsible for developing the Manufacture Royale des Gobelins.
(Cabinet des Estampes de la Bibliothèque Nationale, Paris.)

Fig. 8 *Marriage of the King* from the series The History of the King *from a cartoon by Lebrun, Gobelins, woven on a high-warp loom in the workshop of Jean Jans the Younger. Wool, silk and gold, 17 ft. 11 ins. x 21 ft. 6 ins. (Mobilier National.)*

Allo Photo

Mansell Collection

Allo Photo

Colbert and Louvois, the Minister of War. In 1683 Colbert died and the King named in his place Lebrun's great enemy, Louvois. Though Lebrun still remained the titular director, it was Monsieur de la Chapelle Besse who directed the workshops in practice.

The financial situation at the Royal Treasury brought about a policy of economy and work on the tapestries. *The History of the King*, which required a lot of gold thread, was stopped. Louvois decided to reproduce the same works in order to avoid ordering new cartoons; these included a whole series of tapestries which are copies of Brussels tapestries belonging to the Crown furnishings; *The Acts of the Apostles*, after Raphael; *The Spoils of War* and *The History of Scipio*, after Jules Romain; *The Hunts of Maximilian*, after Orley, and many others.

The beautiful tapestry, *The Triumphs of the Gods*, also called *Arabesques of Raphael*, inspired Noël Coypel, director of the *Académie de France* in Rome, to create designs which illustrate the æsthetic change at the end of the seventeenth century. The result of this shortage of new cartoons led to the production of an exceptional work which was for more than a century a resounding success. This was known as the *India Hanging* (Fig. 6) and had a curious history. It was reproduced from several pictures given by Prince Maurice of Nassau, Stadtholder of the Dutch Republic, in 1679 to Louis XIV. These pictures illustrate natives, animals and exotic plants painted by two Dutchmen, Frans Post and Albert Eckhout, who had accompanied Prince Maurice on his expeditions to

South America and Africa undertaken on behalf of the Dutch East India Company. Exoticism succeeds in an abundance of plants and animals from 'the Indies' which the artists interpreted in tapestry, no doubt by seeing the live animals in the well-known zoo which Louis XIV had created at Versailles.

Lebrun died in 1690 and Mignard, aged seventy-eight, succeeded him, bringing with him an artistic revolution. He undertook to organise the weaving of tapestries of paintings which hung in the gallery of the Château de Saint Cloud, for Philippe d'Orléans, patron of the enterprise. Mignard stayed only a short while, for in 1694 a financial crisis led to the closure of the workshops for five years.

When, in 1699, the Gobelins workshops reopened their doors, Jules Hardouin-Mansart, Superintendent of Royal Buildings, ordered from Claude III Audran the Younger, a new version of a hanging, *The Triumphs of the Gods* (Fig. 1). This tapestry was a tremendous success and was rewoven throughout the eighteenth century, two hundred and twelve times in all. *The Grotesque Months*, by Claude Audran, introduced the æsthetics of the eighteenth century at the Gobelins even more comprehensively than *The Triumphs of the Gods*. From 1699, Audran worked on the decoration of Château Meudon, home of the Grand Dauphin, son of Louis XIV.

From 1707 or 1708, Antoine Watteau was an associate of Audran and he very probably participated in creating the tapestries for which François Desportes drew numerous animals. The Gobelins workshops officially wove *The Grotesque Months* only once. With the two sets, *Les Portières des Dieux* and *Les Mois Grotesques* by Audran, both in an entirely new style, the eighteenth century arrived at the Gobelins Manufactory, while the end of the reign of Louis XIV coincided with a marked change in the tastes and styles of French society.

Fig. 9 *Summer from* The Seasons *after a cartoon by Lebrun, c.1680. Tapestry designed to hang between windows from the workshop of Lefebvre. Wool, silk and gold, 17 ft. 9 ins. x 10 ft. 4 ins. (Mobilier National.)*

9

Allo Photo

MUSEUMS AND COLLECTIONS

Gobelins Tapestries may be seen at the following:

Austria: Kunsthistorisches Museum, Vienna.
France: Le Mobilier National, Paris (previously called *Le Garde Meuble de la Couronne*). A large number of tapestries woven during the reign of Louis XIV are to be found here, and are on view to the public during special exhibitions.
Louvre, Paris
Also: Château de Fontainebleau
Château de Compiègne
Château de Pau
Château de Versailles

FURTHER READING

World Tapestry by M. Jarry, London, 1969. (Translation of *La Tapisserie des Origines à nos Jours*, Paris, 1968.)
French Tapestry by R. A. Weigert, London, 1962. (Translation of *La Tapisserie Française*, Paris, 1956.)
Evolution de la Tapisserie by G. Janneau, Paris, 1947.
Etat Général des Tapisseries à la Manufacture des Gobelins by M. Fenaille (5 vols.), vols. 2 and 3, Paris, 1903–23.

Boulle,
perfectionist in marquetry

Diana Scarisbrick

2

Fig. 1 (Previous page) **Writing table** by Boulle, 1715. *Made for Maximilian Emanuel, Elector of Bavaria. (Louvre, Paris.)*

Fig. 2 **Decorated mirror back** *attributed to Boulle, $29\frac{3}{4} \times 21\frac{3}{4}$ ins. Made for Charlotte de Saint-Simon, daughter of the author of the Memoires. (By permission of the trustees of the Wallace Collection, London.)*

Fig. 3 **Clock-case on pedestal.** *The motif of Love conquering Time in gilt-bronze derives from a composition by Pordenone (1484–1539). (Versailles.)*

Fig. 4 **Kneehole desk** *in contre-partie. The dominant role of the brace veneer gives this piece a particularly opulent character; expense was never considered by Boulle's patrons. (Private Collection.)*

4

Bulloz

J. Freeman

3

Connaissance des Arts: P. Hinoos

A-C Boulle, son of a carpenter, was to become one of the most influential designers in the history of furniture. Made of inlaid tortoise-shell and brass, mother-of-pearl, gold and silver, his magnificent creations indeed achieved their aim to glorify the Sun King

The name of André-Charles Boulle (1642–1732) is synonymous with furniture of a monumental style and magnificence indicative of the highest rank and largest fortune. Designed for official splendour rather than private comfort, it expresses status just as effectively as the great marble and gilded baroque palaces for which it was designed. Just as Charles Lebrun's intention at Versailles was to create a setting which would exalt the person of the 'Sun King', so Boulle's furniture was conceived in the same spirit.

The partnership between Boulle and Louis XIV began in 1672 when, on the death of the royal cabinet-maker Jean Macé, lodgings and work-shops in the Louvre became vacant. Colbert nominated Boulle as the best cabinet-maker in Paris. Trained as a painter, and already in 1669 employed by the Crown in that capacity, he excelled at architecture, engraving, bronze work and monogram design as well as painting and marquetry. The son of a carpenter, he was related to Pierre Boulle, a Swiss cabinet-maker employed by Louis XIII, so his background, training and aptitude fitted him even at the early age of thirty for the royal warrant. The King did not hesitate. Boulle succeeded Macé and was thus set on the path he was to follow, with his sons, for the next half century; the production of furniture for the royal palaces at the Louvre, Versailles, the Trianon, Fontaine-bleau, Marly and St. Germain. Louis XIV wished to furnish each of these and end the medieval practice of taking his furniture with him every time he changed residence.

The scale of royal patronage meant that Boulle could accept few private commissions, though he is known to have worked occasionally for the Duc and Duchesse d'Orléans, the Prince de Rohan and the bankers Samuel Bernard and Pierre Crozat. Members of foreign ruling families such as Philip V of Spain, the Prince Bishop of Cologne and the Elector Maximilian of Bavaria obtained furniture from Boulle and in 1688 the Siamese ambassadors were given a coffer to present to their Empress

5

6

Giraudon

Giraudon

Fig. 5 *Cabinet on Stand*, c.1670. *Veneered with floral marquetry on an ebony ground using light coloured woods. The crowning feature of the gilt-wood gallery emphasises the architectural character of this cabinet. (Musée des Arts Decoratifs, Paris.)*

Fig. 6 *Wardrobe designed by Boulle. Ebony with gilt-bronze mounts.*
This cupboard combines the charming floral marquetry seen also in Fig. 5 with elegant classical detail running in a band down the centre front. The lions' heads and rosettes which decorate the base are also inspired by antiquity. (Louvre, Paris.)

as an example of the finest standards in French cabinet-making.

The genius of Boulle raised cabinet-making to an art and endowed French furniture with an unmistakably national character. Prior to this, seventeenth-century French furniture consisted of a medley of ideas inherited from Italian and Dutch sources. When Boulle, fired with Lebrun's classical spirit, and responding to the royal sense of greatness, used his superlative technical skills to match the products of the *Manufacture Royale des Meubles de la Couronne* and created furniture in the grand manner, the supremacy of Parisian cabinet-making was assured, and in this, as in the other arts, France assumed the leadership in Europe.

Bérain's delightful grotesques featuring monkeys, chinoiseries and fanciful figures heralded the Rococo

Essential to Boulle's style was his perfection of the technique of brass and tortoise-shell marquetry. These materials had been used by Italians since late in the sixteenth century and the inventories of Cardinal Mazarin and Anne of Austria (Regent and mother of Louis XIV) include

cabinets inlaid with metal, mother-of-pearl, horn and semi-precious stones. At first Boulle used this technique in the rather solemn manner of Lebrun, then, from 1690 after Lebrun's death and when the impulse towards a less formal style had come from the king himself, he collaborated with the designer, Jean Bérain (1639–1711) whose delightful grotesques featuring monkeys, chinoiseries and fanciful figures have a light-hearted character heralding the rococo movement (Fig. 4). The procedure involved the gluing together of thin sheets of brass and tortoise-shell, then the pattern – either a dignified Lebrun arabesque or a charming Bérain grotesque – was set out on a paper pasted on the surface and cut out with a saw. The cut layers were then separated and replaced together to make two types of marquetry: one with a tortoise-shell ground with the pattern of brass, called *première-partie* (Fig. 13) and the reverse, or *contre-partie*, with a shell pattern on a brass ground. Great accuracy and patience was required in the arrangement of these panels, which were then glued as veneers on to plain carcases, usually of oak. The symmetrical character of the marquetry was emphasised by its use for matching pairs of armoires, cabinets and tables, and the first and counterpart panels were also used to decorate the inside and outside of cupboard doors. Those parts of the furniture not covered by the marquetry were veneered in ebony and occasionally coromandel wood. The brass was sometimes engraved (Figs. 2, 9 and 13), and colour was introduced in the form of a foil on which the tortoise-shell was laid, while elements like horn, silver, ivory, pewter and mother-of-pearl were sometimes incorporated into the pattern.

This expensive and elegant technique had one serious disadvantage; for the application of such different substances as metal (silver, brass and pewter) and animal products (horn, ivory, tortoise-shell and mother-of-pearl) on to wood meant that, since each of these reacted differently to varying conditions of temperature and humidity the veneers were constantly lifting from the carcase, itself subject to warping and distortion.

To counteract the fragility of his marquetry, Boulle fixed gilt-bronze mounts to the more exposed parts of his furniture, and these, like his inlay patterns, were of a classical character and combined so splendidly with the flat marquetry panels that their practical purpose was eclipsed. In achieving this alliance between cabinet-making and bronze work, Boulle established the essential features of French furniture right up to the Revolution.

He owed his freedom to combine these techniques, using both metal and wood, to his privileged position at the Louvre which exempted him from the rigid specialisation enforced by the guild system on its members. So considerable was Boulle's sculptural ability that he could model, cast, chase and gild his own bronzes, and consequently the output of his workshop was of the highest quality. Besides mounts for cabinet-making, accessories such as balustrades, grilles, light fittings and fire-dogs were made under his supervision.

Boulle was responsible for both the design and the execution of his furniture

Although Boulle collaborated with Lebrun and Bérain, he also designed independently. There are fine pen and chalk drawings for furniture attributed to him in the Louvre and the Musée des Arts Décoratifs (Fig. 12) and he published a series of engraved designs under the title *Nouveaux Desseins de Meubles et Ouvrages de Bronzes Gravés par André-Charles Boulle*. He was thus responsible for both the design and the execution of his furniture, and much of his impact stems from his superlative sense of style. In the formation of his style, his experience as a collector must have played an important part.

Like Rembrandt, Boulle never missed an auction and had to endure great financial difficulties as a result of his purchases. Among his Old Master drawings were forty-eight illustrations of Ovid's *Metamorphoses* by Raphael, Rubens' travel sketch-book and two hundred drawings by Stefano della Bella of ballet and theatrical performances; his collection of prints covered all the great Italian and Flemish masters and among forty oil paintings was a beautiful Correggio. He owned six thousand medals, wax models by Michelangelo, examples of the work of his great contemporaries, Coysevox, Coustou and Girardon, as well as plaster casts of antique sculpture. The greater part of this outstanding collection was burnt in the fire that

consumed his premises in 1720, so we have little evidence to link his collection to specific examples of his work, though it would seem that the inspiration for the *Marsyas* and *Apollo and Daphne* reliefs on the great Wallace Collection armoires must come from these Raphael drawings (Fig. 11).

An inventory of the stock which perished in this fire gives us valuable information about the range of activities carried out by Boulle and his staff of twenty assistants. Boxes containing wooden marquetry representing flowers, fruit and animals, and pictures of hunting scenes, were burnt, but the record of them proves that his skill as a marquetry worker was not restricted to his tortoise-shell and brass technique. An example of his skill in assembling wood marquetry is the Louvre armoire (Fig. 6). The severe architectural character of wardrobes such as this one, is worthy of the most grandiose conceptions of Lebrun but, since most of them are now only to be seen in the sober setting of museums, it is difficult to appreciate how well they must have harmonised with the great mirrored walls and painted ceilings of Versailles.

Various cabinets of great splendour are attributed to Boulle and he brought this favourite piece of seventeenth-century furniture to a climax before it went out of fashion. He produced versions of the bureau, a piece of furniture that was increasingly in demand as learning was once more considered an occupation for the nobleman. The *bureau Mazarin* was brought up to date with its surface, including eight legs of baluster or scroll form, decorated with Boulle marquetry. Boulle also developed a simple rectilinear table with three drawers in the frieze, of which the centre drawer was recessed and the whole veneered and enriched with gilt-bronze mounts, and this piece, the *bureau plat*, assumed great importance in the following century. Another type, with drawers resting on the top surmounted by a clock, is represented by the bureau of the Elector Maximilian Emanuel, which dates from 1715 (Fig. 1).

The strength of the contemporary literary movement is reflected in Boulle's designs for bookcases with glazed doors, and the current passion for classical antiquity was expressed in the commissions for medal cabinets. Fifteen of these were supplied for Versailles, and five of them are now in the Louvre Collection. The importance accorded to clocks and barometers is indicated by the number of cases designed by Boulle (Fig. 3) as well as pedestal supports (Fig. 13). Boulle *torchères* and *guéridons*, circular trays supported by a thin shaft resting on three legs, were designed to carry candelabra and these were placed on each side of the many elaborate marquetry tables that lined the mirror-clad walls of Louis XIV's great apartments.

The emergence of the commode came as a result of much experimentation by Boulle (Figs. 8, 9 and 10). It originated as a version of the bureau but with fewer drawers which extended the whole width. Sometimes the commode was provided with doors and the top covered in either marquetry or marble. The earliest documented examples are the Mazarine commodes formerly in the Bibliothèque Mazarine, now in Versailles, made in 1708–9 for the King's bedroom at the Trianon (Fig. 9). Here Boulle has applied his marquetry to a curved surface in an attempt to meet the fashion for furniture of a less rectilinear and severe character and, though the inspiration for this piece is the classical sarcophagus,

7

Museum Photo

Fig. 7 *Design for the* **Clock-case** *illustrated in Fig. 3.*
The source is known to us through a print by Ugo de Carpi which may have been in Boulle's collection.
(Musée des Arts Decoratifs, Paris.)

Fig. 8 **Commode.** *The contrast between the tortoise-shell and brass inlay and gilt-bronze mounts combines with the monumentality of design to produce an effect of great sumptuousness.*
(J. de Rothschild Collection.)

Fig. 9 **Commode.** *This historic piece, the earliest documented commode, is one of a pair delivered by Boulle in 1708 for the King's Bedroom at the Trianon. It combines features of the chest with the eight legged support of the desk.*
(Grand Trianon, Paris.)

Fig. 10 **Commode in contre-partie.** *The application of Boulle marquetry to the gently curved surfaces of this piece announces the future development of the eighteenth-century commode.*
(Louvre.)

Connaissance des Arts: J. Guillot

George Rainbird, Ltd.

Giraudon

Boulle Furniture

Fig. 11 **Wardrobe** *attributed to Boulle, 100 x 64 x 13 ins. Veneered with panels of marquetry, the two doors are decorated with classical subjects taken from Ovid's* Metamorphoses: Apollo and Daphne *and the* Flaying of Marsyas. *(By permission of the trustees of the Wallace Collection, London.)*

Fig. 12 **Design for a wardrobe** *by Boulle. Pen and ink wash. From designs such as this, Boulle created his furniture. The structural quality and balance between marquetry and mounts is obvious even in the design stage. (Louvre, Paris.)*

Fig. 13 **One of a pair of pedestals** *possibly from the workshop of Boulle, 50 x 18¾ x 11¾ ins.* Première partie. *Veneered with engraved brass and tortoise-shell with bronze mounts, the upper panel of scrolled foliage contains the interlaced L's of Louis XIV. (Wallace Collection, London.)*

the experimental quality of the design is indicated by the addition of a second set of feet to bear the weight of the drawers and top.

Besides pieces of such importance, Boulle's workshop produced smaller luxurious objects; mirror- and picture-frames, ink-stands and jewel caskets, all using his characteristic marquetry which displays the same dignified spirit and uses the same motifs as his furniture.

His most ambitious achievement was the Grand Cabinet of the Dauphin, completed between 1680–83, which was considered to be one of the wonders of Versailles. Here he was responsible, not only for the furniture, but also for the marquetry frames of the Venetian glass mirrors set in the walls. His parquet floor was a masterpiece of inlay, and included highly elegant monograms of the Dauphin and his wife. Damp caused the rapid dilapidation of this room but an idea of what a Boulle style interior was like can be obtained from a study of the picture at Versailles, believed to be that of the Grand Cabinet de Monseigneur at Meudon.

One of the mysteries of the history of furniture is that Boulle has always been appreciated for, even in the eighteenth century, when his tortoise-shell and brass marquetry was replaced by tropical woods and his classically inspired gilt-bronze mounts and rectilinear forms by carved surfaces and asymmetrical rococo bronzes, pieces of Boulle were regarded with the greatest respect and the day-book of Lazare Duvaux records that Madame de Pompadour collected it. With the classical revival under Louis XVI, cabinet-makers such as Levasseur and Montigny, who had been trained by Boulle's sons, found a ready market for the restoration and imitation of Boulle. Because of its inherent fragility, the majority of the pieces associated with Boulle have been extensively restored. This creates a further difficulty because Boulle did not stamp

his work and some of his followers attained such a high degree of excellence that, unless there is documentary proof, it is often difficult to determine which pieces are original. The Wallace Collection contains a knee-hole desk, veneered in *contre-partie* Bérainesque marquetry which was catalogued as seventeenth-century until cleaning revealed the maker's mark – that of Le Gaigneur, an *émigré* craftsman who worked in the Edgware Road in about 1815.

Admiration for Boulle reached its zenith in Europe in the middle of the nineteenth century and this resulted in a flood of copies and drastic restoration. Because of this, much Boulle has a Victorian flavour which does not commend it to people of taste. It should be recognised, however, that Boulle's achievements were considerable: under the patronage of a king who understood the value of luxury as a means of dominating others, he was able, through his grasp of classical principles, to temper magnificence with restraint and thus give his furniture the quality of greatness.

FURTHER READING
Furniture by F. J. B. Watson, London, 1956. (Wallace Collection Catalogue with introduction and notes.)
Les Ébénistes du 18ième Siècle by Comte François de Salverte, Paris, 1953.
Les Boulle by Henry Havard, Paris, 1892.

MUSEUMS AND COLLECTIONS
Furniture by Boulle may be seen at the following:
London: Jones Collection, Victoria and Albert Museum; Wallace Collection
Paris: Louvre; Musée des Arts Décoratifs

Versailles- a Paragon of Palaces

Sir Charles Petrie

Versailles under Louis XIV was far more than a great palace; it was a glittering social centre and an all-powerful administrative focal-point as well. Dominated by the firm but idiosyncratic hand of Louis, it became the source of artistic inspiration for all Europe

Fig. 1 (frontispiece) *View of the formal gardens at Versailles* by *Jean Baptiste Martin, called 'Le Vieux' (1659–1735).* The gardens at Versailles (1662–90) were laid out by Le Nôtre who was the Contrôleur Général des Bâtiments du Roi. The symmetry of the architecture is echoed in the landscaping of these gardens which provide a perfect complement to the building.

2

Mansell Collection

Fig. 2 *Bust of Louis XIV* by Bernini (1598–1680), c.1665. Marble. Bernini was invited to France in 1665 to redesign the Louvre. Nothing came of this venture but this magnificent bust of the Sun King remains to commemorate his visit. (Versailles.)

The incarnation, and to no small extent the driving force, of the *grand siècle* was Louis XIV himself, and Lord Acton certainly did not exaggerate when he declared that the King 'was by far the ablest man who was born in modern times on the steps of a throne'. He had one gift above all others which stood him in good stead: his perfect manner. He was invariably dignified and reserved, calm and courteous. Louis also possessed the happy knack of saying the right thing at the right moment. When, for example, Condé returned from one of his later campaigns to pay his respects to the King at Saint-Germain, he found the monarch at the top of the staircase surrounded by the Court. Condé, to whom the years had been none too kind, mounted the stairs with difficulty, and when he had done so apologised to Louis for his slowness. 'My cousin', replied the King, 'when one is so heavily weighted with laurels as you are, one cannot walk quickly'. His physical appearance was a further advantage for, with his handsome features and serious, almost phlegmatic, expression, he seemed admirably fitted to play the part of a monarch in that heyday of royalty.

In later years Louis XIV travelled in great pomp, but very little escaped those shrewd blue eyes

Moreover, Louis knew intimately the land over which he ruled. From infancy he had travelled, often in the most uncomfortable circumstances, the length and breadth of France. In the days of the Fronde the King had been driven from place to place as the fortunes of war swung this way or that, and he knew how the ordinary Frenchman lived. He had spent hours talking to the landlords of wayside inns while broken axles were receiving attention; he had sheltered in farm-houses for the night when torrents of rain rendered impossible further progress along a flooded road. In later years he travelled in great pomp, it is true, but very little escaped those shrewd blue eyes. 'Nothing', he said himself, 'is more dangerous than a King who generally sleeps but wakes up from time to time', and he certainly lived up to his convictions in that respect. In the dark days when one army after another was going down to disaster before the apparently invincible Marlborough, and when the very climate seemed to have leagued itself with England and Austria, he knew how it all appeared to the average Frenchman and launched his appeal in language that met with a response in every French heart.

On the other hand, Louis XIV was very susceptible to flattery and became increasingly so with the passage of the years until the disasters of the War of the Spanish Succession brought him back to reality. He was inclined to take for granted that the success of ministers and generals was due to his own inspiration, and the logical consequence of this was the employment towards the end of his reign of second-rate men both in the council chamber and in the field; after all, if the King was the motive power in the State, then the capacity of his instruments mattered little.

This line of reasoning was to cost France dear. Like so many men who are successful, Louis came to believe that things would always be as he wanted them, and he was proportionately the more astonished when he found that this was not the case. He was none too well educated in many departments, and he sometimes joked about his own ignorance; indeed, the circumstances of his youth would in any case have prevented him from receiving a good education in the academic sense. Yet he was avid for information. 'My intention' he wrote in 1663 to Cominges, 'is to be informed of all that is best and exquisite in all countries and in all branches of knowledge, and to make the best of such information for my honour, and service, and glory.'

To the glory of himself in particular and of France in general

The background of the monarchy was Versailles, though the residence of the Court was not definitely fixed there until 1682. It was not only a palace in the sense of, say, Buckingham Palace; it was also a town and the centre of the administration. In effect, it was a Washington. The palace alone accommodated ten thousand people, and in its immediate surroundings fifty thousand more. There was a world of difference between the range of buildings, half-palace and half-monastery, set in the wild Guadarrama mountains by his maternal great-grandfather, Philip II of Spain, and Versailles, set in gardens laid out by Le Nôtre. Philip built the Escorial to the glory of God; Louis built Versailles to the glory of himself in particular and of France in general. Yet in one respect they had much in common, for both constituted a permanent exhibition of national arts and crafts.

At the moment when Louis took the government into his own hands on the death of Mazarin, his country was largely dependent on foreign imports, notably those from Germany, Italy and Flanders. All luxury products came from abroad, and each year there was, in consequence, a loss of currency which impoverished the national exchequer. Louis and his minister, Colbert, were fully aware of the importance of this problem when they set about reorganising the economy of France by stimulating activity in the old royal industries and creating new ones, some of which are still prosperous today. The marble quarries in the Pyrenees, for example, which had not been worked since the fall of the Roman Empire, were opened up again and their products dispatched to the yards of Versailles and the Trianon; the silk industries at Lyons were also developed; and clever propaganda kept Europe informed of the marvels of the new royal residence.

It has been alleged that the King's passion for building was an unnecessary embarrassment

3

J. Freeman

Fig. 3 *Louis XIV and His Heirs*
by Nicolas de Largillière
(1656–1746).
None of the royal family
represented here with the King
actually acceded to the throne.
His son, standing behind the
seated King, his grandson on the
left and his eldest great-
grandson, the small child, all
died before Louis himself. The
Duchesse de Vent-Adour, on
the right, was governess to the
royal children.
(Wallace Collection, London,
By Permission of the Trustees.)

Fig. 4 *Louis XIV as a child,*
mid seventeenth century.
Bronze, height 2 ft.
Louis XIV acceded to the throne
at the age of five, in 1643.
(Louvre, Paris.)

Fig. 5 *La Chambre du Roi at*
Vaux-le-Vicomte by Le Vau and
Lebrun, 1657–61.

4

Connaissance des Arts: R. Guillemot

5

Connaissance des Arts: R. Guillemot

Fig. 6 **The Building of Versailles** *by Van der Meulen (1632–90). The building of Versailles began in 1669, when the King appointed Le Vau to head a brilliant team of painters, sculptors, architects, decorators and gardeners to create this magnificent setting for his Court. The palace alone housed ten thousand people. (By Gracious Permission of H.M. The Queen.)*

6

7

Giraudon

8

Scala

Fig. 7 **Louis XIV receiving the Ambassador of Spain,** *from the tapestry series* History of the King, *Manufacture Royale des Gobelins, seventeenth century. (Versailles.)*

Fig. 8 *Le Salon de la Guerre at Versailles designed by J. H. Mansart, Lebrun and Coysevox, begun 1668. Dedicated to the glory of war, the central medallion of starkly white marble depicting the King as a triumphant victor dominates the whole room.*

to Colbert's financial policy, but if one takes the long-term view, as Louis himself certainly did, it is difficult to sustain this argument. The money was nearly all spent within the country, and the construction of the various palaces was in the nature of a scheme of public works which gave employment to discharged soldiers in time of peace. No doubt Louis might have been content to proceed on a more modest scale, but what he built has since justified its cost many times over.

At any rate, the policy was overwhelmingly successful. The reign of Louis was the apogee of France and her wonderful civilisation. Her soldiers were supreme in the field; her diplomacy was at its most brilliant; her art and letters had few competitors. The result of this pre-eminence was felt in all quarters and in all countries. The Court of

Louis XIV attracted visitors not only from Europe, but also from Africa and the East, and the influence of Versailles can be seen in the ruins of the Summer Palace of the Manchu Emperors in China.

There was not a petty German prince who did not feel impelled to imitate, so far as his resources would permit, the pomp of the King of France. This led at times to extravagances which can only be described as absurd, and the story is told of more than one princeling who provided himself with a French mistress; yet what civilisation there was in Germany, in the century that followed the desolation of the Thirty Years' War, owed its inspiration to France.

It was the same in Italy, where French influence made itself felt early, although for a long time Spain had been the dominant power. By 1665,

Italians had begun to wear wigs in imitation of Louis, and for the rest of his reign his imprint on the manners and customs of the country became ever more steadily marked.

As for England, no more than the rest of Europe had she been able to resist the attraction of the French Court, and from the Restoration of Charles II onwards, an ever-increasing stream of French ideas and modes of life flowed into the British Isles. In the field of letters, Addison was the pupil of Boileau, more gifted, more refined and more brilliant than his master but never forgetful of his teaching. Moralist, satirist and critic, a poet equally at home in the romantic, allegorical and tragic styles, he could turn with ease from French wit to English humour, and often seems to blend the two. Then there was Alexander Pope, who owed much to France in his earlier days; his moral poems have the precise turn of wit characteristic of Boileau, and he represents, as it were, the transition between Boileau and Voltaire. Even the Highland chieftains aped the manners of Versailles, and at the Battle of the Boyne in far-away Ireland the commands on both sides were given in French. It was indeed a notable achievement.

At the same time, few institutions have provided so much amusement for subsequent generations as the Court of Louis XIV with its elaborate etiquette, though it is difficult to see why this should be the case. Perhaps at first sight it is not too

Fig. 9 *Louis XIV playing Billiards* by A. Trouvain, 1694. Engraving.
Billiards was first introduced as a game in 1598 in England. It was immediately popular and was a favourite pastime at the French Court.

easy to repress a smile at the spectacle of the heads of ancient families clamouring for the privilege of helping the King on with his shirt or off with his breeches; of ladies taking mortal umbrage because others were allowed to sit in their presence; and of the world of social importance which separated a chair with arms from one without. When, however, one looks a little closer, it is to realise that these regulations were not as stupid as they appear. The upper classes in France, as elsewhere at that date, may have been chivalrous, but they were without manners, and the only way to prevent them from behaving like savages was to prescribe a rigid code of behaviour. How necessary this was can best be realised by comparison with their utter lack not only of restraint but even of common decency whenever the

opportunity occurred. For example, at a court ball in connection with the marriage of the King's grandson, the Duke of Burgundy, one of the leading nobles was caught in the act of stealing a diamond clasp from the bride's dress.

Gambling and every sort of expensive dissipation was encouraged

As in everything Louis did, there was method in the apparent extravagance of the Court. His aim was to wean the nobility away from the provinces, where they had for centuries been so powerful, to ruin themselves at Court. When this had been accomplished he gave them sinecures and pensions which rendered them dependent for their very existence upon the Crown against which their fathers had so often rebelled. Thus gambling and every sort of expensive dissipation was encouraged, and the spending of money became almost a test of loyalty. In 1705 Louis, after planting his grandson on the throne of Spain, wrote to his representative in Madrid concerning the Spanish aristocracy, 'You must preserve all the external prerogatives of their dignity, and at the same time exclude them from all matters on which their knowledge would tend to increase their reputation'. This was certainly the policy which was pursued in France and which, carried to excess in the two succeeding reigns, did much to precipitate the French Revolution.

Louis did not, however, allow etiquette to stand in the way of merit. One of the very few who were admitted to his private apartments was Racine, and he did not hesitate to ask Molière to lunch with him. It was, indeed, the great age of French literature, and the King certainly played his part in its encouragement. As had been her lot in the thirteenth century, so again in the seventeenth France was unanimously acclaimed the intellectual sovereign of Europe, all eyes being turned towards her and all ears listening for her action. It has been alleged by the King's critics that everything which is celebrated was effected in the first half of the reign, but the fact that Racine did his best work during the latter half of the period is sufficient answer to the charge. In addition, the later years of Louis could still boast such theologians as Bossuet, Fénelon, and Bourdaloue; such philosophers as Malebranche, Bayle, and Fontenelle; such mathematicians as L'Hôpital and Varignon; and the great botanist Tournefort, to name but a few of the leaders of French intellect.

Any account of the *grand siècle*, however brief, must make some mention of Colbert, one of the greatest statesmen France has produced. His greatness lay in the fact that he saw his country's problems clearly, and as a whole. He gave £50,000 to the Paris observatories and £160,000 in pensions to men of letters, among whom were Pierre Corneille and his brother, Molière, Racine and Perrault, as well as many eminent foreigners, of whom some at least belonged to countries with whom France was from time to time at war. In all these activities Colbert worked in close co-operation with Louis, so that even if the King's direct encouragement of literature and art has been over-emphasised there can be little doubt that Louis personally must take a great deal of the credit for the triumphs made in those fields during his reign.

UNPRETENTIOUS ELEGANCE IN FURNITURE

Douglas Ash

Fig. 1 **Armchair**, *French, second half of the seventeenth century. Gilt-wood and satin brocade. Turned legs were often replaced at this period by legs such as these of square section. There was also a growing interest in upholstery. (Musée des Arts Décoratifs, Paris.)*

Fig. 2 **Invalid chair**, *French, first half of the seventeenth century. Upholstered walnut. The back of this rather ungainly but useful chair is hinged, and can be adjusted to any angle by means of the ratchets at the sides. (Musée des Arts Décoratifs.)*

Museum Photo

Museum Photo

Fig. 3 *Folding stool*, *French, second half of the seventeenth century. Upholstered walnut. (Versailles.)*

Overwhelmed by the magnificence of the furniture made for the royal Court of Louis XIV, it is easy to overlook the simpler pieces which were more dependent on line and fine carving for their effect and were produced for the middle classes in seventeenth-century France

It would be easy to consider the furniture of the reign of the Sun King looking only to the cabinet-work of the brilliant constellation of designers and craftsmen established in the Louvre and at the Gobelins. But this would take into account only one sector of contemporary production, a sector, moreover, which was confined to the Court and the wealthier aristocracy. It is with the more widespread and practical objects of general use that we are concerned here.

One must realise that there was not, strictly speaking, a single Louis XIV style; indeed, it is sometimes the habit in France to refer to all furniture from the accession of the first Bourbon sovereign, Henri IV, in 1589, to the assumption of personal power by Louis XIV in 1661, as being in the 'Louis XIII style'. It is ironic that the philistine Louis XIII was not in the least interested in any of the applied arts, but that many elements of design from his reign persisted long after the accession of his son at the age of five in 1643. Henri IV had taken a lively interest in artistic development, but as this interest manifested itself

Fig. 4 *Guéridon, one of a pair, French, second half of the seventeenth century. Carved wood with marble top, height with base 40 ins. (Musée des Arts Décoratifs.)*

5

Fig. 5 *Easy chair 'en confessional', French, after 1673. Carved walnut, upholstered in Utrecht velvet.*
Volute arms of this sort are known as os de mouton, *or ram's horns.*
(N. Landau Collection, Paris.)

6

Hamlyn Group

7

Museum Photo

8

Museum Photo

Fig. 6 **Table**, *French,
seventeenth century. Oak.
The frieze is carved in low relief
to imitate a fringed cloth.
(N. Landau Collection.)*

Fig. 7 **Table**, *French, second half
of the seventeenth century.
Gilt-wood and marble.
A new, more luxurious, type of
table.
(Musée des Arts Décoratifs.)*

Fig. 8 **Day-Bed**, *French, end of
the seventeenth century.
Gilt-wood and satin brocade.
(Musée des Arts Décoratifs.)*

partly in the installation in the Louvre galleries of privileged craftsmen including Flemish joiners, it resulted in the perpetuation of the already powerful influences from the Netherlandish portion of the old Duchy of Burgundy.

These influences were reinforced when Marie de' Medici, Regent of France during the minority of Louis XIII, introduced Rubens and other Flemish artists to the French Court. Under Richelieu, the worldly and crafty prince of the Church who governed France in the name of the King, aesthetic conceptions from Italy exercised increasing sway. This process continued under Cardinal Mazarin, who was himself of Italian origin. He succeeded Richelieu in 1642 and was thus already in the saddle when Louis XIV became nominal king. He imported craftsmen from his

native Italy and his enormous personal collections of objects of fine and applied art included examples from many other European countries and even China.

It is evident that all these outlandish aesthetic forces, meritorious though they may have been, must have held the French inventive spirit in such servitude that some powerful factor of almost revolutionary strength was essential to free it. This factor was the death of Mazarin in 1661 and the King's consequent determination to manage without anyone faintly resembling an *éminence rouge* and to direct the destinies of France in areas which might expand his own prestige.

Up to this time, French furniture had changed little since the death of Louis XIII. Twist-turning – a variety of turning used for the decoration of chair and table legs – had been in use since the first quarter of the century. It persisted, though to a lesser degree than previously, and might even be found on the stands of luxurious cabinets, in combination with other details of a more sophisticated kind. Diagonal stretchers on legged furniture also retained their popularity. In France this constructional detail was commonplace in the first half of the seventeenth century and continued after 1700, often, as before, with some kind of turned finial at the point of intersection (Figs. 1 and 10). The earlier type of stretcher in the form of the letter H continued as well (Fig. 5).

Chairs 'en confessional' concealed the face of the user behind one or other of the wings

Despite the persistence of various details, however, there was a gradual change in seating furniture in particular. The many turned knobs on framework of the mid seventeenth century gave way to a simplified treatment involving slender balusters of simpler outline; smooth-flowing scrolls repeated on the supports for the arms which curled forward in pronounced volutes known as *os de mouton*, or ram's horns (Fig. 5); and legs in the form of square-section fluted pedestals capped by mouldings, often with the profile of mushrooms (Fig. 1). At the same time, there was a greater interest in upholstery on chair-backs (Fig. 13). These were generally rectangular, occasionally with an arched cresting, though this was more frequent later. In about 1670 appeared the upholstered wing easy-chair, known as 'en confessional' because the face of the user was generally concealed behind one or other of the wings. The wings were of the usual shape but, in the early stages of development, jutted out from the sides of the top in a rather sudden fashion and were not continued down to the arms as was the case later on. The arms of early examples were open as on most other armchairs, but increased comfort was provided by padding on the upper surface (Fig. 5).

Another type was devised for invalids or for those who merely liked to have a rest without resorting to a day-bed. The back of this type was hinged so that it could be let down to any angle required by means of a ratchet on each side. Precautions were taken against the complete collapse of the back by the provision of two iron rods passing from the back through the length of the arms and emerging in front. The forward end of each rod terminated in a

Fig. 9 **Table**, French,
seventeenth century. Gilt-wood
and marble.
(Musée d'Art et de Céramique,
Narbonne.)

Fig. 10 **Armchair**, French,
seventeenth century. Carved
walnut and satin brocade.
(Musée des Arts Décoratifs.)

Fig. 11 **Bureau Mazarin**,
French, style of Louis XIV.
Walnut.
Writing desks became
increasingly popular at this time.
(Musée des Beaux Arts, Poitiers.)

knob which prevented its being pulled right
through the arm. When such a chair was being used
for normal sitting the protruding rods did nothing
to improve its appearance, but they provide
evidence nevertheless of increased design-
consciousness in the second half of the seventeenth
century.

When the visible parts of the timber of a chair
were intended to be polished, they were nearly
always made of walnut; but if they were required
to be gilt, oak was generally used, though
gilding on walnut was not unknown. The wood was
first given a smooth coating of gesso to provide a
homogeneous surface for the gold-leaf.

The scrolled formation of various members has
already been mentioned. Most early examples of
legs designed in this manner were in a moderate

curve, concave at the top and convex at the bottom
(Fig. 13). In the latter part of the seventeenth
century these curves were found reversed with
increasing frequency (Fig. 5), and in this departure
from the existing convention we can see the
beginnings of the cabriole leg, which had existed
in China for several centuries in fully-developed
form. In the 1690s this type of leg began to occur
on appropriate furniture of all kinds and eventually
established a norm which remained valid throughout the succeeding century. As the mature cabriole
leg came into fashion, the tendency to cover the
seats and backs with woven split cane became almost
universal, and at the same time backs became
lower and stretchers were dispensed with, so that
the prototypes of the styles of the eighteenth
century were already in existence by 1700.

Bedchambers were of great importance as reception-rooms

Day-beds had been known in England at least
since the early sixteenth century, but there are
few surviving French examples dating from before
about 1680 (Fig. 8). The form of the legs and
stretchers followed that of contemporary chairs
and the same could be said of sofas (canapés),
though the latter recommended themselves rather
more in elegant surroundings and were remarkably
sophisticated by the end of the seventeenth century.
Before the death of Louis XIV in 1715 they had
become supremely graceful and well-proportioned,
with luxurious but tasteful carved decoration in
which the scallop-shell, a motif of prime importance
for a decade, began to be replaced or augmented
by foliage and broken scrolls which sometimes
appear as a prophetic foretaste of the Rococo.

It is unfortunate that there is so little
evidence regarding beds of the period and so few
survivors, for bedchambers were of great

Fig. 12 *Carved panel, French,*
c.1643.
This elegant panel was executed
for the Arsenal under Maréchal
de la Meilleraye, who was Grand
Master of the Artillery in 1643.
(Musée des Arts Décoratifs.)

Fig. 13 *Chair, French, late*
seventeenth century. Gilt-wood,
upholstered in Utrecht velvet.
A great interest in upholstering
chair-backs in the seventeenth
century made possible simple
chairs of great luxury.
(Musée des Arts Décoratifs.)

12

13

importance as reception-rooms. It is clear, however, that beds with visible posts were not greatly esteemed in fashionable circles; a type without front posts and with the tester supported by thin chains from the ceiling was preferred, while the structural members of the others were merely considered as an essential framework for the display of rich, monumental draperies.

Despite their limited comfort, upholstered stools continued to be used in vast numbers by nearly every section of French society. These were similar to the lower parts of chairs. Contemporary engravings of interiors often show groups of them ranged side by side along the walls of rooms and generally outnumbering the chairs. The passage of time does not seem to have lessened their popularity, and their design, with few exceptions, always evolved parallel with that of their larger relatives.

Tall cupboards, or *armoires*, sometimes in two stages but generally with a pair of long doors running from top to bottom, took on an altogether simpler aspect. Cornices projected less than before and often had a wide, curved cresting suggestive of a segmental pediment. With noticeable frequency the front corners were rounded, a feature which scarcely appeared on English case-furniture before the Victorian era. Before the death of Louis XIV, the device of backing glazed cabinet-doors with ruched cloth was already in use, though when this treatment was applied to *armoires* it was often confined to the upper half.

Similar changes occurred in French tables as in English, though a great deal earlier. For a few years after 1661, important tables were long and narrow, with H-stretchers, thick columnar or baluster legs and ball or bun feet. They were mostly stoutly constructed of oak and continued to be used in the provinces long after they had ceased to be fashionable among the wealthy. They were intended to stand in the centre of a room or up against a wall, those destined to remain in the latter position often having two or more drawers in the frieze and sometimes a wide apron-piece or ornamental member in the centre which might be carved in low relief to look like fringed and patterned cloth (Fig. 6).

Small tables, however, were far more numerous. From quite early in the period they achieved great elegance, while there was a growing incidence of veneered tops, decorated with elaborate marquetry in symmetrical designs of strap-work, scrolls and flowers. When curvaceous legs began to appear on chairs the supports of tables assumed a similar form. When the reversal of the earlier curves evolved into the cabriole shape and the legs on the opposite side were left straight so that the table could be placed close up against the wall, the result was the console table. By the turn of the century these objects had begun to take on something of the sumptuous aspect which characterised the work of the great designers of the royal Court, and in addition to the scallop-shell motif and scroll-work many had apron-pieces occupied largely by realistic masks in high relief.

Terminal figures carved in the round and disposed at graceful sinuous angles

At the same time, French console tables might have supports consisting of terminal figures carved in the round and disposed at graceful sinuous angles, and the tops of more expensive examples of this kind were sometimes of marble or scagliola (a substitute for marble) instead of plain or inlaid wood (Figs. 7 and 9).

The evolution of certain other pieces was a matter of decorative techniques deriving from the court designers rather than of basic form. An example is provided by the writing-table known as a *bureau Mazarin* (Fig. 11). This had drawers on each side of a central knee-hole, supported on two sets of four legs, the styles of which evolved in the same manner as chair legs.

One type of bureau had a hinged flap which could be let down in the front to form a surface for writing; but in most cases the top was used for this purpose, and these may be considered as the ancestors of the later *bureau-plat*, a writing-table with a flat top and drawers beneath.

FURTHER READING
Meubles et Ensembles Epoques Louis XIII et Louis XIV by Yvonne Brunhammer, Paris, 1966.
Catalogus van Meubelen, Rijksmuseum, Amsterdam, 1952.
Le Style Louis XIV by Henry Martin, Paris, 1947.

Museum Photo

Museum Photo

HENTY

'My dear lads . . .'
Words which became familiar to
Victorian boys who read the books
of George Alfred Henty. He wrote
in the stirring days when Europe
was scaling the final slopes to
world supremacy. His tales recall
the golden age of empire, an age
when Britannia ruled the waves
and much of the globe was
coloured red.

'Have you any Hentys?' is a cry familiar to all booksellers. Today there are collectors on both sides of the Atlantic. The tales of George Alfred Henty have become a craze once more.

In their own time their popularity was matched only by their numbers. Between his fortieth birthday in 1872 and his death in 1902, Henty wrote almost a hundred books for boys and many other novels. The weeklies and annuals which he edited or to which he contributed number many more. *The Times* obituary notice of Henty did not exaggerate in claiming that 'he may be said to have written a continuous history of all the wars, great or little, in which England has engaged since the Norman invasion.'

The titles of Henty's books matched the mood of his public. *By Sheer Pluck, Through the Fray, Held Fast for England* are a monument to all that we find forbidding in late Victorian childhood. *'The Dash for Khartoum* will be appreciated even by those boys who do not ordinarily care a dash for anything,' was one typical review. The author's preface with its characteristic opening 'My dear lads . . .' pointed the way to that concept of manliness and self-reliance which found its most obvious outlet in the Boy Scout Movement. Henty recorded that 'I want my boys to be bold, straightforward and ready to play a man's part, not to be milksops. I have a horror of a lad who shrinks from shedding blood or winces at any encounter.' *The Times* warmly approved this attitude: 'In Mr. Henty's stories there is no nervous underview, no imaginings of things which are not there, but the easy writing of a manly Englishman who takes things as they are.'

Behind the Facade

This is the usual image of Henty, the image that he himself preferred. In truth, the outlines of Henty's personality were blurred even in his own lifetime by the character he created for his heroes. Henty was eccentric, vain and choleric; he feared solitude and affected to despise art; he spent his entire life in the search for violent action, caught up in a torment of self-doubt. He sought in his books a simplicity and heroism which he never found in life, despite the range of his experience.

Henty fought in the Crimea, and in Italy under Garibaldi; he served as 'special correspondent' for the *Standard* in the Italian campaign of 1866, in Abyssinia in 1868 and in the Franco-Prussian War two years later. He served in the Carlist War in Spain, in Ashanti, in India and Afghanistan for his paper; he visited St. Petersburg and was wounded in front of Deligrad in the Turco-Serbian War. He visited the Californian gold fields and started a copper-mining company in Canada. At home, he edited the *United Services Gazette,* contributed to innumerable periodicals on subjects ranging from metallurgy to monsoons, and became president of the Savage Club. He was one of the most formidable Fleet Street characters of his time, that 'stiff, dogmatic, pagan old savage', as one of his colleagues described him. Standing six feet five inches tall and weighing over twenty stone, he was an impressive sight in the Ludgate Bar or in the offices of his publishers, Messrs. Blackie.

What to Look for When Buying

His books brought him a considerable fortune, and remained very popular right through to the interwar period: Blackie reprinted most of his stories in a new edition in the 'twenties and Foulsham still produce an abridged version today. The fact that there are so many editions provides one of the main puzzles for

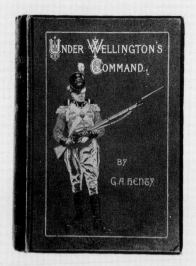

the collector. A few years ago, there was a marked difference in the value of first editions and later impressions or editions; but the task of positively identifying a first is so baffling that later copies have come to have a value which doesn't fall far short of a proved 'first'. The accepted method of identifying a Henty first edition is to compare the date on the title page, if a date is given, with the advertisements at the end of the book. Often what is apparently a first edition will carry the correct date of publication, but a scrutiny of the catalogue at the back may reveal later titles or more often may include the volume in one's hand. In other words, the book had been reprinted with additional advertisements but the title page had not been altered. Quotations from reviews often provide a clue, for Henty was extensively reviewed in most of the literary journals and weeklies.

Henty's books were produced to a standard that was unusually high even for those days. The embossed covers combined decoration, even glamour, with strength to resist some of the hoped-for manliness. Many well-known artists worked on the illustrations, some of which are remarkably fine: Gordon Browne, Wal Paget and Solomon J. Solomans were all noted artists of the day. Today the condition of the individual volume plays a crucial part in determining its value: some early 'firsts' fetch £7 or £8 in a fine state, and only £1 if rubbed or damaged.

A bibliography of Henty's works was produced fifteen years ago by B. L. Farmer, but it is incomplete. A successor is being prepared.

WILLIAM ALLAN

Restoring Paintings

In common with other forms of restoration, that of paintings is highly skilled work, requiring many years of specialised training and practice. It is therefore no job for the amateur, as an unskilled person can easily ruin what might otherwise be a good painting, even allowing for the need for repair.

A typical professional restorer is Mr. Peter Toseland, who works in the Alan Boyle restoration studio in the Brighton Lanes. This studio deals almost exclusively in the commercial restoration of paintings, as opposed to the more scientific and exacting work executed in museums and galleries.

Mr. Toseland is, in fact, an accomplished painter, having studied fine art and general design at Northampton School of Art and the Royal College of Art. For many years, he held two one-man exhibitions a year, as well as teaching full time. However, since taking up restoration in 1960, he himself has indulged less and less in painting and has given only a few exhibitions.

Mr. Toseland's first point was that the restorer's job is not to improve on the original painting or the artist's style. His purpose is basically to conserve and improve the general appearance of the work without deceiving the viewer. He must, therefore, hide the defects caused by wear and tear in order that they do not detract from the overall effect.

Reasons for Restoration

Why are paintings restored in the first place? This is because of age, or transit damage, or because the canvas may have buckled and torn. Alternatively, the paint itself may be flaking or discoloured, due to the pigments combining with each other and with the varnish. The varnish is, in fact, the principal cause of deterioration, as in time it becomes affected by oxidation, leading to molecular rearrangement and loss of essential volatile oils. Thus, it becomes darker and dulls the actual colours to the eye, giving so many paintings an ancient appearance when in reality, the paint underneath may be almost as bright as new. Settling dust can also affect varnish, as it acts as an agent for dampness, serving all the more to break down its original, smooth consistency. In extreme cases of deterioration there is a condition known as 'clouding' or 'bloom', where patches of the painting appear a misty white. All that has happened here is that the varnish has become affected as described above, becoming very brittle, and has broken up into minute cracks which have gradually spread over the surface.

Stripping the Varnish

Having established as best he can the type of deterioration, the restorer must first strip the varnish. This is done with a number of varnish-soluble solutions, but Mr. Toseland, like most restorers, has his own particular favourite formula. He has to proceed extremely cautiously, as he may strip too much varnish and thus remove some of the original brushwork also. With some paintings the paint will not have been allowed to dry fully before the application of the varnish. This makes the restorer's job doubly difficult, as he often finds the paint and varnish fused together.

A canvas ready for restoration

Peter Roberts

The Alan Boyle studio

Minor Repairs

When he has removed the varnish, Mr. Toseland then repairs any minor damage with a filling compound and roughly tints the area back to its original colour. He then gives the whole painting a thin coat of fresh varnish, isolating the newly tinted parts and any other parts needing restoration. This brings out and highlights the original colour of the painting, enabling him to obtain a perfect match.

Using the minimum amount of paint, he then works into the parts to be restored, taking great care not to overlap the original paintwork. Here lies Mr. Toseland's real skill, as he must endeavour at all times to follow the same style and brush technique as the artist. He must, therefore, be extremely flexible in his approach, and sensitive to the aims of the original artist.

Major Repairs

Some paintings are obviously in need of more than just general cleaning and highlighting. As mentioned earlier, many are torn or split. In this case, a canvas is first removed from its stretcher and then completely relaid on to a new canvas, using special gums that will not affect the paint. Any surface damage is repaired and repainted, using the methods described above.

Split or damaged panels are also re-lined, but the process is more complicated and requires more skill. Firstly, the back of the panel is shaved very carefully of all foreign matter until only a thin layer of wood is left backing the painting. Then a piece of silk serum is laid on, and the whole panel is fixed with special-composition glue on to either a new panel or a stretched canvas.

There are very few training-schemes in this field. The alternative is to be apprenticed to a commercial restorer, as Mr. Toseland once was. He admits that at first it was difficult acquiring the restraint and adaptability necessary for each individual artist's approach; this comes with experience. He found that his natural ability and the demands of the business complemented each other very well, but he still thinks that restoration is more a skill than an art.

He obviously prefers to restore better-quality works, and derives greater pleasure from them. However, as in any other business, he must accept the mediocre along with the quality, particularly as it is the former which is frequently in more need of attention.

Useful books on the subject are: *The Cleaning of Paintings* by Helmut Ruhemann, published by Faber and Faber. *The Care of Pictures* by George L. Stout, published by Columbia University Press. *The Care of Paintings* (French and English), published by U.N.E.S.C.O.   NIGEL DAVIS

Varnishing a painting   **Restoring paintwork**

Fontainebleau Then & Now

Fontainebleau has long been one of the pleasantest and best-known summer resorts in the neighbourhood of Paris. Placed only thirty-five miles from the capital, it is in the centre of a forest and has been **a haunt of kings for many centuries.** Here they built their palaces, filled them with beautiful objects, and retired from the bustle of city life. (See pages 1182-1183.)

The first mention of Fontainebleau as a royal hunting-seat is as early as the reign of Louis VII. **Louis gave refuge to St. Thomas à Becket there in 1169,** at which time the saint consecrated the Chapel of St. Saturnin which was later rebuilt by François I and still stands today.

The palace compound was greatly enlarged in 1269 when Louis XII, known as Saint Louis, founded a monastery nearby for the Trinitarians who already had a hospital in the area. Indeed, so many buildings have appeared with time that Fontainebleau has become **affectionately known as 'un rendez-vous de chateaux', a get-together of palaces.**

The palace was a family gathering place as well as a hunting lodge; Philip IV, Louis X, Philip V and Charles IV were all born there, and Philip IV and V died there as well.

But Fontainebleau did not really come into its own until the reign of **that great monarch and patron of the arts, François I.** He brought together an outstanding group of Italian painters and sculptors, including Serlio, Rosso, Primaticcio, Vignola and Niccolò dell'Abbate.

Cellini also spent a great deal of time at Fontainebleau, where, despite the bitter opposition of François' mistress, Mme.d'Etampes, he completed some of his finest work. He redesigned a doorway which was 'wide and low, in their vicious French style', as he put it. For the lunette above, he sculpted the famous 'Nymph of Fontainebleau' which has come to symbolise the genius and intense creativity of the palace at that period.

Henri IV also spent vast sums of money in decorating what was now far more than a mere hunting lodge, and in 1601, his son, Louis XIII, was born there. **The traditional uses of Fontainebleau, however, were curtailed by the creation of Versailles** by Louis XIV, which cast all other palaces into a secondary role.

Fontainebleau is one of the easiest and most enjoyable daytrips from Paris. By train, it is 1¼ hours from the Gare de Lyon, and by car, 35 miles along the N7 highway. There are also various bus excursions which can easily be arranged by any reputable tourist agency.

The State apartments at the palace are open daily from 10 to 12 and 1 to 5 in summer, and from 10 to 12 and 1 to 4 in winter. The admission of 1 franc is halved on Sundays. The garden and chief courtyards are open all day.

VISITING THE GOBELINS WORKSHOPS

Not surprisingly, the Gobelins workshops are to be found in the Avenue des Gobelins. They have been there since 1601, but this was not the beginning of the story. There was already a royal tapestry factory at Fontainebleau in the fifteenth century. Henri II moved the entire works to Paris, but production was interrupted by the religious wars of the sixteenth century. It was when Henri IV revived the industry in 1601 that it was installed on its present site, which was at that time a dye works belonging to the two brothers Gobelin, standing on the banks of the River Bièvre. The river is now covered by the Rue Berbier-du-Mets.

Colbert's Influence

Renown came to the factory only when Colbert began to take an interest in the arts in the mid-seventeenth century. He called on every branch of the decorative arts to embellish the outward signs of Louis XIV's power, and the Gobelins factory became the emporium of contemporary style. Stage by stage it was expanded. In 1662 Colbert placed the royal carpet factory of the Savonnerie under the same management as the Gobelins works. This factory had been started in 1604 at the Louvre and later moved to a soap works or *savonnerie* at Chaillot, which explains its name. It was not moved under the same roof as the Gobelins —this only happened in 1826—but the two factories were closely linked in all but location. In 1667 Louis XIV added a furniture factory. Other branches produced silver, ormolu, mosaics and anything else which might add to the splendour of the royal household. A final addition to the Gobelins manufacturing complex was made after the Second World War when the workshops of the Beauvais tapestry factory, destroyed by the bombs of the Luftwaffe in 1940, were transferred to Paris.

Weaving

Today, as in the seventeenth century, the tapestries are woven on high-warp looms, several of which have survived from the time of Louis XIV (one is illustrated here). The weavers work on the reverse side of the loom, copying the design from a painting behind them which is reflected in mirrors. So painstaking is the process that the average weaver can only produce about 2-1/5 square inches a day.

The Buildings

The buildings themselves have retained their seventeenth-century look, and give a good idea of the works as they must have been in the days of Louis XIV. There is a modern museum building with a good collection of tapestries, but it is not yet open to the public. The works themselves, however, can be visited on Wednesday, Thursday and Friday from 2:00 to 4:00 pm. Tours can be arranged by the Service des Monuments Historiques and cost 0.50 francs.

Weaving on a high-warp loom at the Gobelins manufactory in Paris. The costume reveals that the engraving is eighteenth century.

Market Trends

VICTORIAN TOYS

London Museum

Toy soldiers by William Britain Ltd.

Victorian Toys have only recently come into focus as collectable antiques. Ten years ago, dolls, dolls' houses, rocking horses and perhaps toy train sets were the only items which made their way into London salerooms and antique shops. Nowadays, there is hardly a feature of nursery life that is not reflected in auctions, from high-chairs to toy windmills, from jigsaw puzzles to miniature sofas.

Toy Soldiers

The most dramatic breakthrough has taken place in the field of toy soldiers. Even chipped and broken items from William Britain's vast range cost well over £1 apiece, and the regular sales at Phillips have demonstrated that some collectors will cheerfully pay £20 and more for rare items which reflect the departed glories of the Empire. Elephant-guns and mountain-batteries now command prices which astonish those dealers who regarded dolls as the *prima donnas* of the saleroom. This tendency to 'male lib' in the saleroom also extends to table-games. Jigsaws, even with a piece or two missing, cost between £10 and £30, and mechanical games and train sets can cost even more. An extremely fine steeplechasing game recently fetched £45, and the same dealer also sold a jigsaw of the Coronation of King Edward VII for £22 in 1971, an average price today.

Children's Books

Children's books, too, are now eagerly sought after. Animals, topographical books and fairy tales are the leaders in the field, partly because so many distinguished artists worked on them. Books illustrated by Arthur Rackham, for example, come second after the tales of G. A. Henty (see page 1239) as the favourite quarry for trans-Atlantic book hunters. They fetch between £7 and £8 as a rule. Henty's novels are now very expensive. At Sotheby's in February 1972, first editions of some of his commoner titles fetched up to £40 and a rare item, *Camps and Quarters*, sold for £620. The works of Henty's later imitators, and the equivalent books for girls, can generally be bought for under £5. Otherwise, the only bargains left seem to be the publications of the various Schools' Associations and the Temperance League.

Dolls and Dolls' Houses

Dolls and dolls' houses are still very expensive to buy. Christie's and Sotheby's both handle a fair number of these items each year, and prices have risen steadily in the past five or six years. A fine dolls' house of the 1860's would certainly move into three figures at auction, and its make-believe tenants can seldom be bought for less than £50.
DAMASCUS HOBNAIL

VICTORIAN ENGLAND

The Collector's Sale at Sotheby's Belgravia in December 1971 confirmed one of the latest trends in antique collecting, the growing interest in Victorian photographs and photographic equipment. Although high prices were paid for talbotypes, daguerreotypes and autograph photographs, the cameras themselves didn't reach that level. The 1890 Instantograph quarter-plate bellows camera, a magnificent affair of wood and brass, sold for only £6, and a 'special' version of the camera fetched only one pound more. In contrast, twenty-one mounted photographic prints, collected together under the title *Pencil of Nature*, sold for £2,500. A fine talbotype entitled *The Chess Players*, dated 1839, fetched £410; and a very interesting talbotype view of Thames barges and the Hungerford suspension bridge sold for £240. These high prices reflect the recognition that collectors are giving to these fascinating survivals, now eagerly sought after by students of both social history and the arts. Even visiting-card portraits and ordinary commercial photographs fetch a pound or more in the antique shops and at the *bouquinistes* of Portobello Road and the British Museum area. All the indications are that this is likely to prove a highly profitable field for the collector, and one which is still relatively unexplored. Early wooden plate cameras are probably the most collectable of the photographic items, and the makers to watch for are Thornton Pickard, Sanderson, and Newman & Guardia.

Commercial Furniture

Victorian commercial furniture, on the other hand, is so plentiful that prices are staying at much the same level as in recent years. A piece needs to have an exceptional pedigree, or some outstanding feature, before it attracts much attention at auction. The products of Maple or Waring and Gillow eighty years ago may seem an unlikely source of either aesthetic or financial satisfaction, but such is the pressure to find new outlets for the collector that there is a marked tendency to dress them up in the formal panoply of an antique.

Cameo Glass

Cameo glass is also widely collected. A fine vase, with a tall funnel neck of a deep turquoise colour overlaid in white, sold for £170 at Sotheby's in March 1971, and two cameo glass scent-bottles—always eagerly sought after—sold for £60 and £50.

Bottles and Vases

Small objects such as scent-bottles and miniature vases are the most eagerly sought-after examples of cameo glass. On the larger pieces the decoration can sometimes be overwhelming; it is perhaps for this reason that the smaller items take precedence in antique shops and salerooms. It is assumed that there is unlikely to be any slackening of interest in these attractive and highly collectable items.
DAMASCUS HOBNAIL

Talbotype of two men sawing and chopping wood, one of twenty-one mounted photographs from Pencil of Nature (1844) which sold at Sotheby's Belgravia in December 1971 for £2,500.

THE AESTHETIC MOVEMENT

Sotheby's Belgravia

A stained pine chimneypiece by Charles Rennie Mackintosh which fetched £70 at Sotheby's in March 1970.

In the field of aesthetic pottery prices tend to reflect the prestige of the manufacturers: thus Minton and Worcester will always fetch high prices. Pieces made at the factories which were established specifically to meet the demand for aesthetic pottery fetch prices generally between £10 and £50 depending on quality and the rarity of shape or ornament.

Dresser Pottery

Pieces designed by Christopher Dresser are more valuable; over £100 has been paid at public auction for an Ault vase designed by Dresser, and his pottery is seldom sold for less than £40.

Pilkington's Royal Lancastrian Lustreware

Pilkington's Royal Lancastrian lustreware is even more expensive. Depending on the artist and the size of the piece, current prices are in the £50-£300 range. A fine Pilkington's Royal Lancastrian vase painted by R. Joyce, with wild animals and grasses in silver lustre on a rusty ground, bearing the date code for 1909, sold for £220 at Sotheby's Belgravia in January 1972. Another vase of a less spectacular design, by W. S. Mycock, fetched only £30 at the same sale. These two prices probably represent the limits within which most prices are likely to move in the coming months. A fine Royal Worcester moon flask with the code for 1883 sold for £115, and a vase and cover by George Owen for £360 at that January sale, reflecting the higher commercial value of Worcester.

Mackintosh Furniture

Furniture designed by Charles Rennie Mackintosh has attracted a growing number of collectors in the past few years and there is every likelihood that the prices paid for his work will increase markedly in the future. The developing enthusiasm for all products of the aesthetic movement has given a fillip to even the simplest of Mackintosh's designs. A pair of chairs, of ebonised oak, with tall ladder-backs and drop-in caved seats, sold for £420 at Sotheby's in 1970, and a similar pair fetched £400 at the same sale. A stained pine chimneypiece designed by Mackintosh for the architects Honeyman and Keppie sold for £70, a rather low figure in comparison with the prices paid for the chairs.

DAMASCUS HOBNAIL

FRENCH FAIENCE AND GOBELINS TAPESTRIES

Like other modern nations which see their past being bulldozed away by the present, France is becoming increasingly anxious to preserve her heritage. Early faience (French tin-glazed earthenware) is now fetching high prices and the buyers are almost invariably French. They understand the subject much more deeply than the English, who express only a minority interest. An exception is a well-known St. Porchaire fruit dish, exhibited at the Victoria and Albert Museum. It is painted with the arms and crown of France, encircled by the Order of St. Louis. When it went through Christie's in June 1937 it made £420; in July 1951 it made £1,102. In the same sale, a pedestal salt cellar decorated in brown, blue and green on a cream ground was sold for £861. Not surprisingly, tin-glazed earthenware of the mid-seventeenth century is exceptionally uncommon. Since most examples are worthy of museum collections, there is every reason to expect that prices will continue to climb.

Later Faience

The faience from the later years of Louis XIV's reign is much more plentiful. A large and rather ugly Nevers polychrome cistern supported by eagle's claw feet and painted with tritons and water nymphs (similar to the one in Fig. 5, page 1220), probably after prints by Pierre Brébrieffe, fetched £65 at Sotheby's in May 1957. More recently, a Rouen *seau á bouteille* painted in vivid blue with typical lambrequin motifs associated with the early eighteenth century made £120. In July 1969, a small Rouen polychrome tureen enriched with chinoiseries was sold for 190 guineas at Christie's.

Tapestry Values

Early Gobelins tapestries are not unappreciated today, but the prices they fetched between the wars have seldom been bettered, if you take into account the ravages of inflation. For instance, five magnificent panels depicting scenes from the conquest of Flanders by the Sun King, after designs by Van der Meulen, fetched £4,095 in April 1924 at Christie's. And yet a complete set of the Twelve Months attributed to Le Blond and woven on a yellow ground realised only £3,400 at Sotheby's in July 1953.

A type of Gobelins popular today is the verdure tapestry. One, mainly woven in shades of blue and yellow, which shows a river landscape bordered by trees with geese and heron in the foreground, made £1,900 at Sotheby's in July 1966. When a tapestry from a well-known series appears on the market, a high price is likely. For example, a panel from the series on the months of the year and the royal residences, depicting May and St. Germain (see illustration), fetched 2,600 guineas at Christie's in July 1969. But it is the condition of the panel which is of cardinal importance to any prospective purchaser. This in itself accounts for considerable fluctuations in price.

TOM MILNES-GASKELL